Lecturer's Manual

Human Resource Management

Fifth edition

Derek Torrington
Laura Hall
Stephen Taylor

ISBN 0 273 65165 X (printed)
ISBN 0 273 65888 3 (web)

An imprint of **Pearson Education**

Harlow, England · London · New York · Reading, Massachusetts · San Francisco · Toronto · Don Mills, Ontario · Sydney
Tokyo · Singapore · Hong Kong · Seoul · Taipei · Cape Town · Madrid · Mexico City · Amsterdam · Munich · Paris · Milan

Pearson Education Limited
Edinburgh Gate
Harlow
Essex CM20 2JE
England

and Associated Companies around the world

Visit us on the World Wide Web at:
www.pearsoneduc.com

Fifth edition published in Great Britain in 2002

© Pearson Education Limited 2002

The rights of Derek Torrington, Laura Hall and Stephen Taylor
to be identified as authors of this Work have been asserted by them
in accordance with the Copyright, Designs and Patents Act 1988.

ISBN 0 273 65165 X (printed)
ISNB 0 273 65888 3 (web)

10 9 8 7 6 5 4 3 2 1

Printed in Great Britain by Henry Ling Limited, The Dorset Press, Dorchester, Dorset

CONTENTS

ACKNOWLEDGEMENTS

We are grateful to the Financial Times Limited for permission to reprint the following material:

A quiet revolution in human resource management, © *Financial Times,* 16 August, 2001; Thriving on the chaos of the future, from FT.com, Mastering Management, © *Financial Times,* 28 September, 2000; Survey – Franchising – Sandwich chain crams a lot in 35 years, © *Financial Times,* 26 June, 2001; Inside Track – Hearts and minds set for recovery, © *Financial Times,* 23 July, 2001; NSH spends £1bn a year on temps, © *Financial Times,* 15 May, 2001; New direction – freelancing means independence, but with a catch, from FT.com, © *Financial Times,* 20 August, 2001; National News: Telework revolution failing to catch on, says TUC, © *Financial Times,* 4 August, 2001; Inside Track: warts-and-all hiring policy, © *Financial Times,* 28 August, 2001; Lies, damned lies and creative CVs, from FT.com, FT Career Point © *Financial Times,* 10 August, 2001; Leadership: Do you have what it takes? from FT Career Point, © *Financial Times,* 15 January, 2001; A greater emphasis on diversity, © *Financial Times,* 10 August, 2001; Certainly not a soft option, from FT Career Point, 22 June, 2001; Emotional intelligence from FT Career Point, © *Financial Times,* 12 December, 2000; An attraction based on similarities, from FT Career Point, 21 May, 2001; A bankrupt idea's great future, from FT.com, © *Financial Times,* 29 May, 2001; Agents for career change, from FT Career Point, © *Financial Times,* 9 May, 2001; A bridge to work's future, from FT.com, © *Financial Times,* 30 August, 2001; National News: Drive planned to preserve compromise on worker rules, © *Financial Times,* 2 August, 2001; A plea for flexibility, from FT.com/In/Health, © *Financial Times,* October 2000; Pandora's pay packet, © *Financial Times,* 14 May, 2001; Employment minister fires the latest shots in equal pay battles, from FT.com, 8 May, 2001; How the rich get richer, © *Financial Times,* 6 December, 2000; Benefits package: Flaws in the perfect work environment, from FT.com, © *Financial Times.*

We are grateful also to the following for permission to use copyright material:

Catharsis with your cards, from The Financial Times Limited, 28 August, 2001, © Adrian Furnham; Putting the team into top management, from The Financial Times Limited, 6 October, 2000, © Donald Hambrick; Inside Track: a bigger picture of performance, from The Financial Times Limited, 7 August 2001, © Neil Britten; and People issues are central to the success of any organisation, © *Irish Times,* 24 July 2001.

USING HUMAN RESOURCE MANAGEMENT IN TEACHING

The text, *Human Resource Management*, 5th edition, is intended to be suitable for self-study as well as for classroom work, so it is presented in way that produces a number of obvious teaching points.

1   The ACTIVITY boxes are included to help the readers review periodically what they have been reading. Do they understand it? Is there some point that will need further exploration through pursuing one or more of the references? These can also be used for on-the-spot discussions with members of the student group to review their understanding and to consolidate their knowledge.

2   TABLES and FIGURES and similar ILLUSTRATIONS can be used as visual aids or as focal points of discussion.

3   SUMMARY PROPOSITIONS can be used both to draw a session to a close and to prepare for the next. We have, however, found that some tutors use them back to front by setting them up as the framework for a lecture/discussion session based on the material in the chapter before the students have read it, or instead of the students reading it.

4   There are full REFERENCES at the end of each chapter. These can be either a starting point for students to develop their work further, or a resource for tutors who may not be fully familiar with the subject matter in some of the chapters. Although the sources are extensive, we suggest that your library should include a number of core journals for student use so that they can keep up to date. You may want to modify this list, but our suggestions are:

>   – *British Journal of Industrial Relations*
>   – *Employee Relations*
>   – *Human Resource Management Journal*
>   – *Income Data Services: Report, Review and Study*
>   – *International Journal of Human Resource Management*
>   – *IRS Employment Review*
>   – *Journal of Managerial Psychology*
>   – *Journal of Occupational and Organisational Psychology*
>   – *People Management*
>   – *Personnel Review*

5   WINDOWS ON PRACTICE are examples from current practice, anecdotes and other types of illustration dropped in to the text from time to time. In teaching these can be particularly useful – and a little dangerous. The usefulness is that there is usually someone in the group who can tell a better story, so they help both participation and examples from current practice. The slight problem is that the teaching point can be overwhelmed in the horror stories, so that students remember the stories, but not the point they were intended to clarify.

6   DISCUSSION QUESTIONS have been introduced in this edition at the close of each of the chapters on strategy or operations. Their purpose is to help people make sense of their *understanding* of the chapter, rather than simply recalling the points made. That is the purpose of the summary propositions.

7   At the end of each part, sample EXAMINATION QUESTIONS are included mainly for illustration, although some could be used as essay topics for examination practice. We have not included outline answers on the website/in the *Lecturer's Manual*. The reason is that the questions come from a variety of sources, most of which do not provide outline answers or marking schemes. If we were to suggest appropriate answers, it could be misleading.

8   Also at the end of each part is a short CASE STUDY that relates generally to the material in the preceding chapters. Suggested feedback is provided on the website/in the *Lecturer's Manual*.

INTRODUCTION TO THE WEBSITE

On the website for the book there are two elements: Student material and Lecturer's material.

On the student side the following is provided:

- Multiple-choice questions covering each chapter of the book which can be attempted and marked electronically as a form of revision.

- Short articles, case studies or exercises linked to each chapter. These substantially increase the amount of learning material provided beyond what is included in the book itself. For each, discussion questions are provided based on the article and/or making links between it and the content of the relevant chapter

On the lecturer side the following is provided:

- A brief overview of each chapter in the book.

- The case studies and articles provided on the student side, together with feedback on the discussion questions.

- Feedback on the seven case studies included at the end of each part of the book.

ORGANISING YOUR TEACHING

We assume that the students' learning will proceed in three separate strands, with constant connections being made, rather like triple helix. The three elements are:

(a) Face-to-face interaction with the lecturer and with other students: TEACHING

(b) Independent study, notetaking, review and reflection by the student: READING

(c) Monitoring of progress and reinforcement of learning, some by the lecturer and some by the student: ASSESSMENT.

The text is obviously used in a number of different ways according to the student group, but is most likely to be organised on a single-semester basis, with two semesters being used to cover the whole subject, although there will also be some singlesemester courses (on MBA introductory programmes, for instance) that will be very selective of the material that is used. We therefore offer various suggested ways of organising the teaching.

Two linked twelve-week semesters

Semester One: Resourcing and Reward		Semester Two: Organisation, Performance and Development	
Week	*Chapter(s)*	*Week*	*Chapter(s)*
1	1 and 2	1	5
2	3	2	6
3	10	3	7
4	11	4	17
5	12	5	18
6	13	6	19
7	14	7	20
8	30	8	21
9	31 and 32	9	22
10	35	10	25
11	36	11	26
12	37	12	27

This approach relies on the 'Strategic Aspects ...' chapters being read by students as an introduction to each section of their work, with their understanding being confirmed in the face-to-face sessions. It also leaves out the six chapters on interactive skills, as we find that these are used in a variety of ways. Some lecturers ignore them altogether, others leave them for students to work on individually at home, and others incorporate them into regular teaching. We have always believed that the best use is either privately by the individual or in a block of teaching time. We strongly advise tutors to include them in the students' learning. Not only do they provide practice in the particular situations, they also are very effective in consolidating learning of the more academic material by making real the processes in which they are embedded.

Single-semester courses

For a single-semester introductory course we suggest an introduction that concentrates on operational aspects, one that concentrates on strategic considerations with some operational features, or one that is essentially practical in its approach. The selection of topics will depend greatly on the interests of the lecturer and the nature of the student group. Here are our suggestions:

Introductory course: operational emphasis

Week	Chapter
1	1
2	3
3	5
4	10
5	12
6	14
7	18
8	20
9	25
10	32
11	35
12	36

Introductory course: strategic emphasis

Week	Chapter
1	1
2	2
3	3
4	6
5	9
6	16
7	21
8	24
9	26
10	29
11	34
12	38

Introductory course: practical emphasis

Week	Chapter
1	1
2	5
3	8
4	11
5	14
6	15
7	18
8	23
9	25
10	26
11	33
12	38

CHAPTER 1 THE NATURE OF HUMAN RESOURCE MANAGEMENT

Chapter 1 aims to provide a broad introduction to the study of human resource management. We start with a few paragraphs focusing on contemporary change in the workplace and the structure of work as a means of illustrating the significance of 'people management' in today's organisations. The next section tackles the thorny issue of providing a definition for the term 'human resource management'. We argue that the term is commonly used in two distinct ways; as a way of describing a particular management function responsible for the achievement of organisational objectives and as a means of describing a specific approach to the management of people. In the latter case, HRM is presented as the most recent in a long line of phases in the historical development of people management. The earlier phases are briefly described, and this is followed by a somewhat longer section reviewing debates about the recent HRM phase. The chapter ends with a section setting out the philosophy of HRM that underlies the rest of the book.

Additional teaching material

The following article by Richard Donkin is taken from the *Financial Times* website. It takes forward a number of the ideas discussed in Chapter 1, providing a good basis for a seminar discussion or an assignment. Discussion questions together with some suggested answers are provided at the end.

A quiet revolution in human resource management

By Richard Donkin, *Financial Times*, 16 August 2001

Is human resource management beginning to undergo one of its periodic transformations where the job, or job title, mutates before our eyes and adopts a different and possibly more exotic appearance? It happened in the 1980s and 1990s when the title 'personnel manager' almost imperceptibly faded from the calling cards of its most senior professionals. Like an improved soap powder with a biological ingredient, HRM, equipped with something called strategy, promised a new set of tools and measures to reward, motivate and organise employees in the re-engineered workplace. Then, suddenly, there was the internet and teleworking and concerns for 'work–life balance'; and there were difficult employees who wanted gap years or freelance arrangements and more interesting pay deals with the opportunity to take equity. Why did they have to spoil everything?

It was Peter Drucker, the management writer, who identified employees as a specific resource – a 'human resource' – in his 1955 book, *The Practice of Management*. Drucker was at the forefront of those who were attempting to understand the social implications of the large corporation. But he was not alone. In the same year Sloan Wilson was writing in his novel, *The Man in The Gray Flannel Suit*, about the way corporate executives were prepared to bury their emotions and values in the name of corporate conformity. The very next year William H. Whyte identified these individuals as 'the dominant members of our society' in a book he called *The Organization Man*.

'When a young man says that to make a living these days you must do what someone else wants you to do, he states it not only as a fact of life that must be accepted but as an inherently good proposition,' wrote Whyte. His observation is recalled by Daniel H. Pink in his new book *Free*

Agent Nation, which, as the title suggests, describes a quite different proposition that he argues is beginning to transform the US employment contract.

Based on hundreds of interviews with freelance workers across the US, Mr Pink's book outlines the way organisation men like Walt Fitzgerald, a former manager at General Electric, took early retirement in the 1990s, then hired themselves out as a consultants. Mr Fitzgerald's daughter, Theresa, did not wait for any reorganisation before she gave up her own management job in a design department. She returned to her first love – designing – as a freelance in preference to managing other designers. Her father too had been a good artist, studying under Norman Rockwell before his management work made painting impossible. As Mr Pink points out: 'Walt may have led a Norman Rockwell life – but what he wanted was the life of Norman Rockwell.

'The problem for people like Walt Fitzgerald is that, until they were confronted with a radical corporate reorganisation and redundancy programme they were unwilling to confront the possibility that there was life outside the corporation. But the 1990s witnessed a discernible transition in the way many people began to view their so-called permanent jobs and the associated risks in leaving them. Bob Milbourn, a former loan officer in a San Francisco bank, told Mr Pink how he sensed that the risk of one day losing his job was expanding, the longer he stayed. 'For the longest time I was terrified of being laid off,' he said. 'Then I got to the point where I hoped they would lay me off. Then I asked to be laid off.'

Mr Milbourn is one of thousands who have made the break. Mr Pink estimates – he says it is a conservative estimate – that something like 33m Americans today are 'free agents', representing about one in four of the US workforce. This means the US economy now has about 15m more freelance workers than it does manufacturing workers. The number of freelancers also outnumber the 20m government employees in the US.

Role reversal

He is not alone in believing that the employment relationship with the employer is undergoing a form of role reversal. In a special section on work in the summer issue of the *European Business Forum* magazine, the academics John Kimberly, Hamid Bouchikhi and Elizabeth Craig, founders of the Executive Careers Institute, argue that 'social and demographic trends point to significant changes in the traditional configuration of power'.

They write: 'Centuries ago, Copernicus realised that the Earth revolves around the Sun, not the reverse. In management we may be in the midst of another Copernican Revolution, a revolution in which the relationship between the firm and the employee is inverted, and in which the "customised workplace" replaces the hierarchical, military-inspired model that has served so long and so well.'

The comparison suffers in one respect – the Earth had always revolved around the Sun whereas the transfer of so much power to the worker would appear to be an unprecedented development. An element of workplace democracy or co-operation may, however, have an ancient history. The late Marijas Gimbutas, an archaeologist, described a pan European Neolithic civilisation that flourished in 'uninterrupted peaceful living' between 6500 and 3500 BC. She believed she had found evidence of a settled social order in which men and women had equal status. If she was correct in her beliefs – and today archaeologists are digging for new evidence to shed more light on her interpretations – we might need to question some of the assumptions we maintain about the inevitability of hierarchy.

No matter, as Daniel Pink has pointed out, thousands of people across the world are promoting their own alternatives and this may be the catalyst for yet another change to the shape of HRM. The institute academics, writing in *EBF* magazine sense the emergence of something called Human Capital Development around what they call the customised workplace. 'The customised workplace,' they write, 'is built on the recognition that to be successful, companies will increasingly have to be organised around individuals rather than the reverse.' Human Capital Development, they argue, is designed to handle the different needs of individuals. The prospect sounds a nightmare for existing human resource departments but, if they're clever, they might greet the idea like a bugle call from the Seventh Cavalry. As it is human resource management has been undergoing a tough time from line managers who seem to be increasingly resentful of its methods.

Only this week, a Gallup poll blamed HR ideas such as competency frameworks and 360-degree appraisals for growing disenchantment among workforces in the UK. But maybe the real reason behind workplace unhappiness is the clinical atmosphere of the re-engineered post-merger corporation and the way it is breeding disaffection among the young.

Michael Lewis has chartered some of these emerging attitudes in his new book, *The Future Has Just Happened,* where he examines the way people are finding much greater freedom to develop their talents on the world wide web. Open sourcing, a phrase that relates to free accessibility to computer programmes, is becoming an ideology that is being extended into other spheres such as the music business, agriculture and the human genome that are challenging existing concepts covering intellectual property.

If human resource management fails to make sense of such developments its future may begin to look bleak. But then again, it would not be alone among the managerial disciplines and assumptions that could founder in a radically changing workplace. When asked about the future of managers in a free agent world, Daniel Pink says: 'Most managers are toast'.

Free Agent Nation, How America's New Independent Workers Are Transforming The Way We Live, by Daniel H. Pink, is published by Warner Business Books.

The Future Just Happened, by Michael Lewis, is published by Hodder & Stoughton.

European Business Forum is a print and online publication that gives a European perspective on management issues, www.ebfonline.com.

Richard.Donkin@ft.com. Copyright © The Financial Times Limited, 16 August 2001. Reproduced with permission.

Questions for discussion

1   Summarise in a few sentences the main argument being put forward in this article in so far as it relates to the human resource management function.

2   What would be the main implications for the HR function if 'customised workplaces' were to become the norm?

3   What arguments can be advanced to support the view that the 'role reversal revolution' envisaged in this article will not materialise in practice?

Feedback

1   *Summarise in a few sentences the main argument being put forward in this article in so far as it relates to the human resource management function.*

The article focuses on the views of several HR professionals, consultants and writers who have argued that organisations are soon going to be forced to alter their whole approach to the management of people.

Currently, as well as in the past, terms and conditions of employment are largely set by employers on a collective basis. All employees are treated alike and are expected to accept these as a condition of working for the organisation concerned. HR policy and practice are determined centrally and apply to all employees.

These writers are arguing that this model is in the process of changing and that we are moving towards a situation in which individual workers are a great deal more powerful. They will increasingly be able to determine their own terms and conditions of employment and will only work for employers who accommodate their needs.

The term 'customised workplace' is used to describe this new kind of organisation.

2   *What would be the main implications for the HR function if 'customised workplaces' were to become the norm?*

In a customised workplace the central objectives of the HR function would remain the same (i.e. staffing, performance, change management and administration objectives). However, the methods used to achieve these would be wholly different, and they would have different priorities.

First, everyone would be employed on individually negotiated contracts of employment, in the same way as most senior personnel currently are. There would thus be less emphasis in the HR role on central determination of organisation-wide conditions of employment. There would be fewer general rules, fewer set hours of work, a multiplicity of payment arrangements and a reversal of power relationships in the organisation.

Second, staffing objectives would become more important than is generally the case at present. Organisations would have to sell themselves harder at the recruitment stage, and get used to the idea that selection is a two-way rather than a one-way process far more than it has been traditionally. Effective staff retention would become particularly important, because there would be no expectation of loyalty from employees. They would only stay for as long as it suited them and on their terms. Ensuring that this was the case would become the central purpose of HRM.

3   *What arguments can be advanced to support the view that the 'role reversal revolution' envisaged in this article will not materialise in practice?*

As is shown in the article, the customised workplace is already with us, but it is only available to individuals who are particularly talented (and thus in great demand from different employers), very senior (and thus in a position to determine their own working conditions), or working in a very tight labour market (e.g. some IT people).

For customised workplaces to become the norm for the mass of employees much would have to change. The major requirement would be for all labour markets to become very tight, making it very difficult indeed to recruit and retain staff. For this to happen we would need to reach a state in which full employment was sustained over a number of years. It can plausibly be argued that this is unlikely to occur. Jobs themselves would also have to become a great deal more specialised and knowledge based, requiring much more training for people to perform adequately. This would make it sufficiently difficult to replace a leaver to force a change in the power balance at work.

Moreover, employers would have to be in a position where they had no alternative but to respond to the tight market by creating a customised workplace. They are likely to look for alternatives wherever possible, because a customised workplace is likely to be less profitable than a traditional one. They are thus likely to respond by:

- Exporting jobs (i.e. relocating operations to countries where the market is less tight).

- Importing staff (i.e. bringing in hard-to-recruit people from overseas).

- Reducing reliance on the hard-to-recruit groups (i.e. bringing in less highly skilled people to do much of the work).

These kinds of strategies have been used extensively in recent years where labour markets have become tight (e.g. teachers and NHS staff in London and the South East). Recruitment and retention crises have not been addressed by creating customised workplaces because they are too expensive and hard to control. Instead alternatives have been sought.

CHAPTER 2 CURRENT ISSUES IN HUMAN RESOURCE MANAGEMENT

Chapter 2 is new to the fifth edition of the text. With Chapter 1 it forms part of an overall introduction to HRM; only here the focus is on the major contemporary issues and debates rather than on the meaning of terms and their historical development. We have identified what seem to us to be the key issues for students of HRM at the turn of the twenty-first century, especially those which are revisited many times elsewhere in the book. The topics covered are increased competition, globalisation, technological innovation, the development of employment law, the future role of trade unions, the issue of ethics in HRM and the ever-present tension between 'best practice' and 'best fit' prescriptions in HR thinking. The following article takes us beyond the present with a view of likely management trends in future decades.

Additional teaching material

This article by Daniel Muzyka is the first of three on the *Financial Times* website looking at the future of management and management research. Here the author focuses on what he sees as the major contextual factors that will affect management practice in the near future. The article could be used as the basis of a class discussion, student presentation or assignment. Suggested discussion questions, together with feedback, are provided below the article.

Thriving on the chaos of the future

By Daniel Muzyka, *Financial Times*, 28 September 2000

Dr Daniel F. Muzyka is dean of the Faculty of Commerce and Business Administration at the University of British Columbia (Vancouver), where he is also a professor of management. He was formerly IAF Professor of Entrepreneurship at Insead.

How can we describe the last few decades in business? For those of us who have witnessed developments since the 1960s, the words of Charles Dickens come to mind: 'It was the best of times, it was the worst of times.' The past few decades have not only given rise to discussion of chaos and uncertainty, but have given new meaning to these words.

For managers, the time has been one that has tested and exposed the inadequacies of many cherished assumptions and practices. For entrepreneurs, these turbulent times have led to significant opportunities. For those of us monitoring and trying to make sense of the scene, it has been at once interesting, challenging, humbling and exciting.

As humans, we search for ways to communicate and clarify what is happening around us. There are many characterisations of the evolving environment that border on the banal. Take two examples. The internet created a 'new economy' straining against the 'old economy'. (We are beginning to realise these distinctions are overblown.) The introduction of the personal computer would 'liberate' people from central structures and would decentralise the economy. (We are more decentralised in some ways, but have become increasingly dependent upon centralised standards and suppliers.) While these events have created opportunities, none of the characterisations has endured, nor have they had the impact expected. Their failure begs the question: 'what is going on?'

Modern times revisited

So what fuels our turbulent times? Are they more turbulent? There are simple and complex answers to the first question. Accelerating human discovery has led the parade, fuelled by a growing population, the emergence of new economic regions and the growing acceptance of Adam Smith's gospel around the planet. This has fuelled a doubling of scientific knowledge every 17 years, according to a 1997 study.

Another force we can point to is the changing expectations of this growing population. Clearly, there is a greater sense of self-determination, an expectation of rewards and recognition for efforts expended, and a growing appetite for a better life. These forces are interacting in complex ways to move and change markets, businesses and the economic fortunes of regions.

We have enhanced the ability of these forces to affect us by removing many of the barriers that protected us in our various corners of the world. The global village has been realised through communications, burgeoning airline networks and significantly reduced economic (Gatt) and social barriers (Nafta, the EU) to commerce and integrated financial markets. Financial resources are readily available globally and move quickly. Shocks can roll through the global economy with frightening speed and opportunities originate from many different points. To those who espoused globalisation in the 1960s, I simply say, 'be careful what you wish'.

Combined with shocks travelling through the system, we find people both more important and more willing to move around. The irony is that automation, on which so many productivity gains have been built, requires people to create and sustain it. Individuals are more important because of the knowledge they possess and the fact that more of our economy is based on services: the production assets are people and not machines. At the same time, labour mobility in many parts of the world, or at least the opportunity for it, has increased.

Labour is often more willing to travel or move for a number of reasons. First, our expectations of what life should offer have changed. Modern communication and air travel make it easy to shop around and compare lifestyles. Second, the loyalty that joined the person to the corporation has broken down. As corporations have evolved new models for changing times, they have experimented with extensive downsizing and re-engineering.

Such practices, in particular the wholesale elimination of jobs, have fundamentally altered the bonds between a corporation and its staff. People will often stay less for reasons of loyalty and more for the value they perceive their association will generate for them. The combined impact of these factors makes forecasting the future harder: the conditions that existed in the past are less likely to lead to successful prediction than ever before. In the end, the world is more turbulent than in past decades.

Is there any prospect for a reduction in turbulence and uncertainty? The answer is a clear 'no'. We haven't begun to see the effect of discoveries in areas such as quantum computing and the human genome. In recent years, Moore's law, which predicts a doubling in computer chip capacity every 18 months, was surpassed and we are beginning to make headway with some formerly intractable diseases, such as some cancers.

Yet we have clearly not settled socio-economic questions that confront the new global economy: 'how do we deal with the growing rift between rich and poor?'; 'how do we fund key social needs in an era of low taxation and reduced government?'; 'how do we ensure equity of business treatment of the population and consumers in all countries?'; and 'how do we create sustainable economic growth?' These still lie ahead of us and addressing them is critical if we are to build a sustainable relationship between corporate and social needs.

Business reality

So, what is different about business? The reality is that opportunities, in the form of business products and services, don't last as long. Opportunities are neither equally available, nor available in the same way for everyone. Increased complexity is at the heart of this. For instance, people have many ways of managing their schedules, whether it is a diary, hand-held device, database on the web, or personal computer software. It is safe to say that many substitutes exist and more will evolve.

Another reality is that business is generally more 'atomistic' and the boundaries more open and flexible. What does this mean? Companies are being created to exploit more-focused opportunities and working around a smaller set of activities while subcontracting many more. The value chains of some companies look like a piece of Swiss cheese, with the holes filled by suppliers and partners.

This is driven by the difficulty of being competitive in all business activities and the fact that flexibility is gained through subcontracting or strategic partnerships. This trend has led to a position where many e-commerce retailers never even touch a product; their inward and outward supply chains are totally outsourced.

Business is certainly more ephemeral. Research by population ecologists, who study corporate mortality rates, has suggested shortening lifetimes for organisations. Businesses might never have been planned to last forever, but today's environment guarantees obsolescence on an increased scale. This means we move with increasing haste to create and exploit value or we increase our ability to exploit opportunities.

Copyright © The Financial Times Limited 2000. Reproduced with permission.

Questions for discussion

1   Briefly summarise the main argument Muzyka puts forward in this article.

2   What is the relevance of its conclusions for the practice of HRM?

3   To what extent do you agree with the argument being put forward and why?

This is the first of three articles by Daniel Muzyka on the future of management and management research. You may find it useful and interesting to read the others at the FT.com website. They are located on the 'Mastering Management' pages.

Feedback

1   *Briefly summarise the main argument Muzyka puts forward in this article.*

Muzyka identifies a range of separate factors which have come together to form a business environment which is radically different from that which has dominated in the past two centuries. The implication is that we are in the process of entering a new era in business terms and that this requires new thinking on the part of managers.

The article stresses the importance of turbulence in the new era. A picture of the future is painted in which small, flexibly managed organisations are brought into existence to exploit specific short-term business opportunities. Their life cycles will be short and their forms very varied.

The turbulence originates from three distinct but interrelated sources:

(i)   the advance of new technologies;

(ii)   globalisation;

(iii)   changing attitudes among people as regards both work and lifestyle choices.

2   *What is the relevance of its conclusions for the practice of HRM?*

Several points can be made here. First, there is the idea that HRM practice in inherently unstable organisations is likely to be different from that in stable ones. Ways need to be found of motivating people and securing commitment to an organisation that can provide few or no long-term prospects and which is likely to be a risky commercial proposition. This is very difficult to do when other organisations are still offering a degree of job security and career development opportunities.

Second, there is the question of speed of change. If the article is correct in its prognsis we are going to see technology accelerating considerably faster than is currently the case. New opportunities are going to arise very quickly, providing a brief window of time in which they can be exploited. This will mean less time (if any) for systematic planning and more 'seat of the pants' HRM. The pace at which activities will have to be carried out (recruitment, selection, training, etc.) will quicken, leaving little time for the evolution of considered employee relations or performance management practices.

Third, there will be increased pressure on all staff to work flexibly. Competition will require that hours and duties are irregular, with knock-on effects for the administration of contracts and payroll. There will be many different kinds of contract (part-time, temporary, consultant, sub-contracts, etc.), leading to a situation in which it is the full-time, permanent job which is atypical.

The fourth factor which stands out in the article is the contention that people generally are looking for more exciting, dynamic and pleasurable lives. They are increasingly uninterested in stability, notions of loyalty/duty, and less respectful of hierarchies. On top of this, they will soon have global opportunities to develop themselves. The implications for HRM include a need to motivate positively (as opposed to the use of negative tools such as discipline or the creation of fear of redundancy), and more generally a need to work harder at improving job satisfaction.

This points to a need to treat people as individuals rather than as part of a collective employee body, and to be seen to do so.

3   *To what extent do you agree with the argument being put forward and why?*

It is quite possible to be sceptical about the kind of 'brave new world' vision being advanced in this article. Several points can be made to support such scepticism. Some are as follows:

(i)   There is an assumption that technological advancement is going to continue accelerating at the same pace and in the same direction as it has in recent years. The possibility of wars, natural disasters, recessions, etc. are not countenanced in the analysis.

(ii)   There is a belief that people are going to embrace the turbulent environment and cope enthusiastically in a working environment. There is little evidence for this contention. Such evidence as there is, for example in UK universities, suggests that competition for the permanent posts is very keen, particularly among those employed on a fixed-term basis.

(iii)   The vision outlined appears to assume that all industries and all organisations will have to change radically in order to thrive in the new turbulent environment. This is questionable. There will still be industries which remain marginally affected or in which change will come in a more planned, evolutionary fashion. There will also still be industries in which competitive advantage rests, in part, on the fact that change does not occur and where customers can be sure to get an established, traditional product or service (e.g. upmarket restaurants, hotels and shops).

CHAPTER 3 STRATEGIC HUMAN RESOURCE MANAGEMENT

The concept of strategic HRM is a key foundation stone of an HRM approach. However our understanding of strategic HRM has changed considerably over the past 20 years, and this chapter reflects recent thinking in the area. The chapter begins by exploring the move from a mechanical view of a physically existing HR strategy to our current understanding of the value of a strategic *approach* and strategic *thinking.* We go on to explore the different types of connection there may be between organisational strategy and HR strategy.

The bulk of the chapter, however, focuses on three key theoretical perspectives on strategic HR. Two of these perspectives have a longer history and they reflect the general debate in HRM as to whether there is one best way to approach HRM ('best practice' or universalist approach) or whether HRM should be entirely dependent on and made to fit different organisational strategies (contingency or fit approach). The third perspective on strategic HRM which we discuss is based on the resource-based view of the firm. This perspective is more complex, but is critically important as it links with other key recent thinking in HRM generally (for example in the area of learning and knowledge management).

The chapter concludes with a brief review of the role of the HR specialist in strategic HRM. For more information on this aspect see, for example, Hall and Torrington (1998) in the reference list of the chapter, and articles in *HRMJ* and *Personnel Review.*

Additional teaching material

The following article by Michael O'Leary was published in the *Irish Times* in 2001. It discusses the results of a survey of Irish HR professionals. Their chief concerns are identified as are the most significant issues that they say they face. The discussion questions we provide at the end require students to consider the practical consequences of these in terms of HR strategy. Lecturer feedback is provided below the article.

Commercial Report: People issues are central to the success of any organisation

By Michael O'Leary, *Irish Times*, 24 July 2001.
Michael O'Leary of the HRM Recruitment Group writes about some of the interesting findings from a recent survey of human resources professionals.

For better or worse, the Irish employment market has irrevocably changed over the last five years and with it the relationship between employers and employees.

People issues are now recognised as being central to the success of any organisation and, as a consequence, human resources has assumed a higher profile. Few companies in the last five years held any sort of senior management meeting without addressing concerns around staffing levels, recruitment, management development and retention.

Prior to this, how many companies could say that these issues featured often enough on meeting agendas? HR now needs to be firmly aligned with wider business strategy and the relevant practitioners must be central to their organisation's efforts at optimising the value delivered by its employees. In May, HRM Recruitment Group commissioned a unique survey of Ireland's HR profession.

The National Human Resource Practitioners Survey 2001 sought to identify the main issues and trends in HR in Ireland and to look at the people responsible for meeting the significant HR challenges that all organisations face. A cross-section of 500 HR professionals from Irish industry and public service were invited to participate. Completed questionnaires were received from 253 respondents.

Traditionally in Ireland, the HR or personnel function has not featured with the same prominence as within UK or US-based counterparts; 30 per cent of respondents highlighted their function's biggest weakness as 'lack of resources'. Unusual when you consider that in many global organisations, the chief executive officer will often come from HR or at least have spent some time within that department.

For several years Guinness chiefs came directly from the HR function. Some 50 per cent of survey respondents highlighted that, were they not pursuing their careers in HR, they would choose general management, 15 per cent would choose operations while 10 per cent would currently be working in marketing.

The most important people issues for over two-thirds of Irish organisations for the future remain the ability to hire and retain the right people.

Developing 'strategic leadership competencies' and 'customer focus' within the organisation are next. Amongst the biggest challenges to achieving HR goals, respondents highlighted 'keeping line managers focused on HR issues' (29 per cent) and 'resistance to change' (22 per cent).

Survey participants identified 'relevance to core business' and 'HR's understanding of key business issues' as presenting the greatest opportunities for the profession over the next five years while nearly two-thirds cited the 'outsourcing of HR activities' as the greatest threat.

The survey seems to suggest that the combination of pressure to recruit and the scarcity of key personnel over the last few years has resulted in some compromise amongst hiring companies. Respondents were asked: 'If you could change the employees in your workforce tomorrow, how many would you change?' A surprisingly high number (78 per cent) indicated that they would change 25 per cent to 50 per cent of their employees. Only 12 per cent suggested they would make no changes.

Retention remains a critical issue for HR practitioners. Some 43 per cent of survey participants felt that failure to retain key staff has a high impact on organisation performance. Only 4 per cent suggested no impact while 3 per cent of respondents estimated the annual cost of staff turnover as being in excess of £1 million, and 32 per cent indicated that their staff turnover costs could be between £100,000 and £500,000. Perhaps surprisingly, given the costs involved, the survey reveals that over a quarter of organisations do not even calculate the cost of staff turnover.

The survey highlights the three most effective methods for retaining employees in the longer term as being 'management effectiveness through coaching and feedback', 'providing continuous learning opportunities' for employees and the 'culture fit between organisation and employee'. Retention bonuses were seen as the least effective method, identified by only 5 per cent of respondents.

High performance organisations of the future will be determined by the ability of HR practitioners to design credible and effective HR strategies, and by the ability of organisations to recognise HR needs through their full implementation.

A copy of the survey results is obtainable by emailing the author: michael.oleary@hrm.ie Michael O'Leary is managing director of the HRM Recruitment Group, the recruitment and HR solutions company. All material subject to copyright.

Copyright © *Irish Times* 2001. Reproduction courtesy of the *Irish Times*, Dublin.

Questions for discussion

This article suggests that HR now needs to be firmly aligned with wider business strategy and that the relevant practitioners must be central. This brings out two strategic issues:

1   HR practitioners need to be involved at a strategic level and yet the professional function, it is argued, lacks prominence and resources. In such a context what can practitioners do to become more central at a strategic level?

2   In some cases HRM can be strategically aligned with the business but there may be no HR specialists involved in this, or no HR specialists may be employed. Does this matter?

Feedback

This article suggests that HR now needs to be firmly aligned with wider business strategy and that the relevant practitioners must be central. This brings out two strategic issues:

1   *HR practitioners need to be involved at a strategic level and yet the professional function, it is argued, lacks prominence and resources. In such a context what can practitioners do to become more central at a strategic level?*

Students need to focus primarily on the issues facing business at this time in this context – for example the high number of employers unhappy with a large number of their employees, strategic leadership competencies, customer focus and retention issues. Students need to identify key areas for improvement, e.g. selection techniques, and offer expertise to solve problems. Other aspects of a strategic role, such as networking, may be mentioned.

2   *In some cases HRM can be strategically aligned with the business but there may be no HR specialists involved in this, or no HR specialists may be employed. Does this matter?*

Students may argue either way. In some senses it does not matter, as long as there is someone such as the Chief Executive to promote the importance of people issues. On the other hand these people may have the enthusiasm but not the skills and expertise. If HR is outsourced there is the problem of culture fit.

PART I CASE STUDY FEEDBACK

As we are only just getting started, this case can only be handled at a fairly superficial level, and may be unsuitable for inexperienced undergraduates. The main things to look for in answers are:

(a)   The degree to which they have picked up on the idea of *costs* and timetable.

(b)   Their understanding of some of the terms: line, strategic initiative, empowerment (which they should understand) and single union agreement, performance management and Investors in People (which some of them may understand).

(c)   The degree to which they present their ideas in line with the three aspects of the brief given by members of the board.

CHAPTER 4 STRATEGIC ASPECTS OF ORGANISATION

In this chapter we focus on the different forms of organisational context in which a human resource management function, of whatever size or nature, operates. We start by introducing the key structural variables (organisational form, degree of centralisation, etc.), before going on to look at the consequences for management in terms of organisational co-ordination, planning and communication. The particular issues relevant to international organisations are also highlighted and discussed.

Additional teaching material

The following case study focuses on the reshaping of the UK government following the 2001 general election. The discussion questions at the end invite students to compare and contrast organisational management in the worlds of government and business, and the role of Prime Minister with that of Chief Executive.

The re-elected Prime Minister

In June 2001 there was a British general election that re-elected the Labour Party and the sitting Prime Minister, Tony Blair, by a large majority. This was the first time that a Labour Prime Minister had been confirmed in office by the electorate. On previous occasions they had been elected on their policy promises rather than on their performance in office. The day after the election Mr Blair began to set up the organisation of his government. His large majority in the House of Commons gave him considerable power as well as great authority in relation to his elected party colleagues. He also had the great advantage of having spent four weeks touring the country and hearing what people had to say about the previous four years of Labour government.

His initial job was to review the *structure* of government and to appoint Members of Parliament to run the various departments. Some large ministries were reshaped and several had a name change to emphasise a change in their mission. In the previous government members had been appointed to office largely on the basis of their political opinions and their service to the Labour Party. In his tour of the country, many people had expressed to Mr Blair varying levels of disappointment about what had actually been achieved in the previous four years, so now he resolved to ensure that his new government was made up of people committed to objectives and able to deliver what had been promised. Track record in office became more important than service to the Party.

Mr Blair was also concerned – as were other political leaders – at the small number of people who actually voted, barely half of the eligible population. This was widely attributed to the fact that many people saw the proceedings of government as largely irrelevant to their lives.

Mr Blair's organisational task was therefore in two complementary parts: structure and culture. First he had to be satisfied that the various ministries and other units making up the government machine were the right grouping of resources and expertise for the objectives that had to be achieved in 2001 and beyond rather than from 1997 to 2001. Furthermore he had only one chance to get that right. Having reshaped government departments, it would be counterproductive and hugely expensive to change them again during the lifetime of a single parliament. Within a very few days that work was complete: the die was cast.

The cultural aspects of Mr Blair's organisational task were to achieve the right, shared and accepted understanding of what the government had to do, and then to motivate all members to deliver. This was not something to be put in place within a few days, but something requiring regular reiteration, relentless communication and some reworking as it evolved, with constant monitoring and listening.

Questions for discussion

1   Mr Blair had power and authority for his organisational task because of his large parliamentary majority. What incidents might give the Chief Executive of a commercial organisation that type of power and authority?

2   What are the means of evangelisation available to a Prime Minister that would not be available to the commercial Chief Executive?

Feedback

1   *Mr Blair had power and authority for his organisational task because of his large parliamentary majority. What incidents might give the Chief Executive of a commercial organisation that type of power and authority?*

Authority for a Prime Minister comes from being endorsed by the voters. Rarely do Chief Executives have anything like such a powerful democratic endorsement. Power for a Prime Minister comes from being the only person empowered to make the sort of political appointments that his colleagues crave. Apart from a relatively few Scots and Welsh, there is no other British government in which to serve, so all 413 Labour MPs are totally dependent on Mr Blair to satisfy their aspirations for high office. It is also Mr Blair who can also dismiss people from office without notice or the possibility of a claim to an employment tribunal. Nearly all Chief Executives deal in a labour market which would provide attractive alternatives for colleagues.

A Chief Executive would rarely have the same degree of power and authority, but some of the following could help:

-   Having considerable product or market expertise, like Bill Gates or George Davies.

-   Having personally delivered a major business coup that keeps the business viable and employees' jobs secure. Dianne Thompson of Camelot would be an example.

-   Furthering the careers of individuals in the business.

-   When the business is under threat in some way, everyone will support initiatives to lift the threat, provided that the Chief Executive is not seen as the source of the problem.

It could be worth referring back to this question after studying Chapter 6.

2   *What are the means of evangelisation available to a Prime Minister that would not be available to the commercial Chief Executive?*

- Access to the media that will surpass that of any Chief Executive. This is an excellent way of reaching those whom the Prime Minister wishes to influence directly, but also the electorate as a whole on whom they all depend.

- Proceedings in the House of Commons, where the Prime Minister regularly performs with the enthusiastic vocal support of colleagues.

- You could have useful discussion about the identity of the 'apostles'. Are these other senior ministers or spin doctors or sympathetic journalists?

CHAPTER 5 PLANNING: JOBS AND PEOPLE

In this chapter we seek to identify how traditional manpower planning has been developed into human resource planning. In doing this we have not only used the traditional manpower planning framework for analysing and reconciling demand and supply of employee numbers and skills, but we have also incorporated the softer aspects such as attitudes, behaviours, culture and systems. We have tried to balance the statistical and softer aspects. In the chapter we refer to a worked example which is included here and on the student website.

In the chapter we also consider the nature of strategic planning in relation to strategic thinking. We identify the differences between these two strategic aspects and activities and make the connection between strategic HR planning as covered in this chapter and HR strategy as covered in Chapter 3.

Additional teaching material

The following case study is the worked example referred to in Chapter 5. Here, specific activities are suggested, together with some further activities which involve students relecting on planning and related issues in their own organisations. It might be possible to ask students to undertake these activities ahead of a teaching session, to give the material a practical context.

HR planning at the City Hotel

The City Hotel is located in the middle of a medium-sized city. It caters mainly for business trade during the week and for holiday trade during the weekends and in the summer. In the summer and at weekends there is, therefore, a greater demand for catering and waiting staff as there is a greater demand for lunches. During the same periods there is a lesser demand for housekeeping staff as the customers are mostly longer stay. The hotel has been gradually improved and refurbished over the past five years, and trade, although reasonably good to begin with, has also gradually improved over the period. There are plans to open an extension with a further 20 bedrooms next year.

Note 1

There has been a particular problem in recruiting kitchen assistants, waiting and bar staff. This is partly due to local competition, but also to the fact that early starting and late finishing times make travel very difficult. Often there are no buses at these times and taxis are the only available transport. One or two hotels in the area have begun a hotel transport system, and the City Hotel management have decided to investigate this idea in order to attract a higher number of better-quality applicants. A second problem has been identified as the lack of availability of chefs and receptionists of the required level of skill. It is felt that the local colleges are not producing potential staff with sufficient skills, and therefore the management of the City Hotel have decided to consider:

1 A training scheme, run either internally or in conjunction with other hotels.
2 Better wages to attract the better-trained staff from other employers.
3 Investigation of other localities and the possibility of providing more staff.

Note 2

Having mapped the environment, the hotel management looked at the demands and responses for each priority area. For 'customers' the beginnings of the list are shown in Table 5.1.

Table 5.1 Demands and responses for the 'customer' factor

Customer demands	*Responses*
Polite staff	Our staff pride themselves on being courteous
Staff understand that we are busy	We will make procedures quick and simple, people and staff will respond to needs immediately
Sometimes we need facilities we have not arranged in advance	We will be flexible and enthusiastic in our response
And so on.	

Note 3

The management of the City Hotel decided that one of their key objectives over the next three years was to become known for excellence in customer service. This was seen as a key tool to compete with adjacent hotels. Managers used brainstorming to identify the staff behaviours that they wanted to see in place, and summarised their ideas in the format in Table 5.2.

Table 5.2 Behavioural expectations chart: organisation goal – excellence in customer service

Behaviours needed	*How to create or reinforce*
Address customers by name	A customer service training course to be developed
Smile at customer	A group incentive bonus to be paid on basis of customer feedback. Customer service meetings to be held in company time once per week
Respond to requests, e.g. room change, in positive manner	
Ask customers if everything is to their satisfaction	
Answer calls from rooms within four rings	
And so on.	

In addition to this a suggestion scheme was instigated to collect ideas for improvement in customer service. A payment of £50 to be made for each successful suggestion.

Note 4

The City Hotel management has plans to open a 20 bedrooms in a new extension during the coming year. On the basis of this simple model the additional staff required could be worked out as follows:

- 55 bedrooms requires 60 staff.

- The ratio of staff to bedrooms is therefore 1.09 staff per bedroom.

- If the same relationship were maintained (i.e. without any economies of scale) the additional number of staff needed would be: 20 bedrooms × 1.09 staff = 21.8 extra staff needed. Thus total staff needed = 81.2 full-time equivalent (FTE) staff.

Note 5

The managerial staff at the City Hotel exercised judgements on the following human resource planning matters:

1 Management considered the probable reasons for the relationship between people demand and time. It was felt that this was most probably due to the gradual improvement in the hotel over the last five years. Since this improvement had virtually reached its potential it was felt that the relationship between employee demand and time would change.

2 Judgements had to be made on whether the occupancy of the new wing would immediately justify all the additional staff to be appointed.

3 The management considered that since the weather had been very poor in the preceding summer, the bookings for the following summer period might be slightly down on the last year and this shortfall might not be made up by increasing business trade.

4 Judgements were made as to whether staff could be better utilised, with the effect that the additional numbers of staff projected might not be so great.

Note 6

The managers of the City Hotel decided to encourage greater staff flexibility and interchangeability. This interchangeability would be particularly useful between waiting duties and chamber duties. At the present time waiting duties are greatest at the weekend and least during weekdays, whereas chamber duties are the other way around. The effect of this is that waiting staff and chamber staff both have a number of hours of enforced idle time, and the feeling was that there was some overstaffing. By securing flexibility from staff (by paying a flexibility bonus) it was felt that the smooth running and efficiency of the hotel would be considerably increased. It was calculated that the 9 chamber posts and 8 waiting posts could be covered by 16 combined posts (all FTEs).

Note 7

Managers of the City Hotel assessed the levels of customer service at present by collecting questionnaire data from both staff and customers and conducting a series of interviews with staff. They also asked in what areas service could be improved and asked staff how this might be achieved. As well as specific targets for improvement, they found many examples of systems and organisation that did not help staff give the best customer service. Staff understood that getting the paperwork right was more important than service to the customer in checking out and in. The paperwork systems were over-complex and could be simplified. Also, shift-change times were found to correspond with busy checkout times. Plans were developed to improve systems, organisation and communication.

Note 8

The statistical analysis of staff (Table 5.3) was aimed at occupation, age and full-time equivalent (FTE) posts. This analysis was used primarily for three main purposes:

1 FTEs needed to be worked out so that this figure could be used in other manpower planning calculations.

2 To consider the occupational balance of staff and to give information which would be useful from the point of view of staff interchangeability.

3 To plan for future retirements and, in consequence, look at recruitment plans and promotion plans.

Note 9

At the City Hotel 18 staff had left during the preceding year. The annual labour turnover index was therefore worked out to be:

$$\frac{18}{70*} \times 100 = 25.7 \text{ per cent}$$

(*The average number of staff employed over the year is different from the maximum number of staff that have been employed and which it was desired to employ.)

Note 10

At the City Hotel, of the 18 staff that had been recruited over the year, three had been replacements for the same kitchen assistant's job, and two had been replacements for another kitchen assistant's job. The stability index was therefore worked out as:

$$\frac{54}{69*} \times 100 = 78.26 \text{ per cent stability}$$

(*At exactly one year before there were only 69 of the desired 72 staff in post.)

Note 11

A histogram (Figure 5.1) was plotted of leavers over the past year from the City Hotel. It shows how the majority of leavers had shorter lengths of service, with periods of employment of less than six months being most common.

Figure 5.1 A histogram of the lengths of service of 18 employees leaving the City Hotel in the previous year

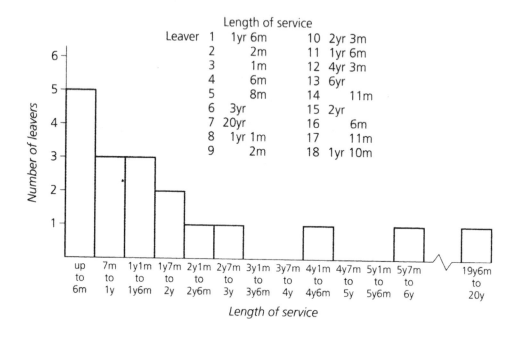

Note 12

Analysis of the age distribution (Table 5.3) indicates that there may be some difficulties with promotions. In particular, a problem was identified for management promotions. There are four general managers, the youngest being 21. In the past such a junior manager would have been promoted after two years' service, which this manager had just completed. The ages of the other managers indicate that there will be no retirements in the immediate future and management staff turnover has, in the past few years, been low. In view of this it was thought likely that the junior manager would leave shortly. This was not desired since this person was particularly able, so ways of dealing with this promotion block were considered, such as creating a new post, which might retain the junior manager's services until a promotion became available.

Table 5.3 Staff by occupation, number and age

Broad occupational group	FTE	Actual number of staff	Ages
General managers and department heads	4 + 5	4 + 5	(45, 43, 30, 21) (51, 47, 45, 35, 32)
Reception/clerical, etc.	7	8	(55, 24, 24, 23, 21, 21, 21, 18)
Chamber staff	9	12	(52, 51, 35, 35, 34, 33, 31, 31, 30, 29, 20, 19)
Porters	3	3	(64, 51, 20)
Chefs	8	8	(49, 47, 41, 40, 39, 24, 23, 21)
Other kitchen staff	12	16	(59, 59, 57, 52, 51, 31, 29, 28, 27, 27, 24, 24, 24, 23, 19, 18)
Bar/waiting staff	10	14	(51, 45, 35, 35, 33, 32, 30, 29, 26, 26, 25, 25, 20, 21)
Handyperson/gardener	2	2	(64, 63)
Total	**60**	**72**	

There are no direct activities relating to this worked example, however there are some associated activities.

Case study activity

Break the students into small groups to begin to prepare a human resource plan based on the information in the City Hotel case study. It is essential that students have pre-read the case and are very familiar with its contents.

Ask groups to specifically design, for the City Hotel, the following in outline:

- supply plan
- organisation and structure plan
- employee utilisation plan
- training and development plan
- performance plan
- appraisal plan
- reward plan
- employee relations plan
- communications plan

Although a number of clues are given in the case study as to activities that can be included in the plan, there has been no attempt to make these complete, to integrate them or to consider the knock-on effects of one plan on another.

The task for the groups is to propose an integrated set of outline plans for the year ahead with an assessment of the financial and other implications supported by a sound rationale.

Specifically stress that each of these plans must not conflict with any of the others and that they should be mutually supportive. Students should be able to describe their plan in about 50 words for each area, as the emphasis is not on the detail but on integration and implications.

Allow plenty of time for groups to discuss, as this is a demanding task. Report back could be in either of two forms:

Option 1

Give each group the opportunity to present their plan to the whole group and allow for time to question and compare different approaches to the same issues. (The groups may have decided to meet in the meantime to do further work.) This timing will be more appropriate to part-time students already employed in the personnel function. For full-time students you may wish to delay presentation until towards the end of the course, and use this as a framework for their ongoing interpretation and application of each session.

Option 2

The case could be used as an individual or group assignment to be presented in written form.

Further activities

1   Work out the annual labour turnover index and stability index for your organisation as a whole. If it is feasible, carry out the same analyses by staff group. Attempt to explain your results. Compare your results with those from another organisation and attempt to explain the differences and similarities. Does action need to be taken, if so what?

2   Analyse the age distribution of either all staff in your organisation or staff at a specific level or in a specific function, depending on what is feasible and useful. Attempt to explain the picture that you find and identify the implications of your findings. Does action need to be taken, and if so what? Compare this with another organisation if possible.

CHAPTER 6 ORGANISATIONAL DESIGN

This chapter tackles the two interrelated issues of structure and culture. Within structure we consider the fundamentals of the organising process – differentiation and integration, – and go on to consider job definition and alternative forms of organisational structure (based on Handy's four forms). After this we review some current trends and issues of organisational structure incorporating smaller size (downsizing, delayering and outsourcing); growth through diversification, acquisition, mergers, alliances and joint ventures; decentralisation and empowerment; business process re-engineering; and the redefinition of organisational boundaries.

The final part of the chapter, on organisational culture, includes a debate on the assumptions on which the concept of culture is based, Schein's model of organisational culture and Martin and Meyerson's critical analysis of different ways of understanding organisational culture. Finally we touch on the ethics of culture change.

Additional teaching material

Here we provide two learning exercises. The first is a case study with discussion questions. Second, we suggest a topic for a class debate.

Exercise 6.1

The following article assesses the organisational structure of the Subway restaurant chain, one of the fastest growing companies in recent years. Subway is a franchise operation, a form of organisation structure which presents specific human resource management issues. Discussion questions, with feedback for lecturers, are provided at the end.

SURVEY – FRANCHISING: Sandwich chain crams a lot in 35 years

By Christopher Swann, *Financial Times*, 26 June 2001

Fred DeLuca, the founder of Subway, the sandwich chain, appears to have the perfect temperament to head a franchise operation.

The softly spoken psychology graduate is remote indeed from the clichés of a control-obsessed chief executive. The sprawling business that he has built up during the past 35 years – and which now claims 15,000 restaurants worldwide – is decentralised even by the standards of a franchise network. Subway franchisees have acquired progressively more power as the chain has grown.

'Many franchise chains want to keep a lot of control at the corporate level,' says Mr DeLuca. 'We think a decentralised structure is a better way to manage the business.' For many years, the group purchased products centrally and distributed them to their franchisees. Now, the franchisees elect their own independent purchasing co-operatives. The group's advertising strategy – which most groups tend to regard as a fundamental prerogative of the central board – has gone the same way.

An advertising agency – whose board members are elected by the franchisees – guides the group's international strategy. On a local level, franchisees elect or nominate a local representative to oversee advertising. Corporate headquarters, meanwhile, confines itself to setting the broad values which underlie advertising. Mr DeLuca appears quite comfortable with the devolved and democratic structure of the business. 'At least half of the time I find I would have done things differently. But this does not mean that I would have been doing things any better,' he says. Running a franchise chain, he says, requires some different skills from managing a centralised company. 'I learned early on that, with a corporate store, I could ask the manager to get the window cleaned and it would be done. With a franchise unit, if you tell them to wash the windows it does not mean they will do it. There is a greater element of persuasion and co-operation involved,' says Mr DeLuca. The franchise model has been crucial to the group's success. In 1975, a decade after Mr DeLuca set up his first store in Bridgeport, Connecticut, there were only 15 Subway restaurants – which was a much slower pace of expansion than the company had projected.

More disturbingly, Mr DeLuca had started to notice an inverse correlation between a store's distance from the headquarters and its sales.

'If we had continued to expand through corporate-owned stores, I imagine we would have remained a regional chain in Connecticut, with no more than 1,000 stores,' says Mr DeLuca. Since embracing the business of franchising, the group has grown at a frantic pace. By 1990, Subway had opened 5,000 restaurants and started to expand into Mexico. Just four years later and it had outlets in Israel, Saudi Arabia, Austria, Brazil and Russia.

Now, Subway is the second largest restaurant chain in the world with 15,000 units in 76 countries and sales of $5bn a year.

A good deal of this success has been due to the growing public interest in health, which has been capping the ambitions of some burger-based rivals.

The chain has always been reluctant to 'play the health card', as Mr DeLuca puts it. 'All the evidence suggested that consumers did not respond to health-based advertising,' he says.

But the temptation was too great when a college student came forward last year claiming to have lost 245lbs by eating nothing more than Subway sandwiches. Jared Fogel has since become a mascot for the sandwich chain, featuring in a series of television commercials and travelling the country to promote the brand. Even before this, however, the company was riding the crest of the health wave. 'People have been increasingly keen to eat healthier fast food for some time,' says Mr DeLuca. 'Not only do we use a lot of fresh vegetables but seven of our sandwiches contain less than 6 grams of fat.' In spite of this boost, Subway has not rested on its laurels. Four years ago, it started to work on adding some new items to its sandwich menu.

This led to the introduction, early last year, of a range of new proprietary sauces and exotic breads. The result was even better than the company had predicted: some store sales rose by about 20 per cent.

This kind of sales growth, the company hopes, will help Subway to expand even further.

On a recent visit to the UK, Mr DeLuca set the goal of matching the number of McDonald's outlets in the UK within 10 years. This would mean increasing the number of restaurants from 55 to 2,000.

Meanwhile, the company has been using the internet to attract new franchisees and now recruits about 50 per cent of its new store owners online.

However, Mr DeLuca is convinced that the success of the Subway model will be the most important factor in realising the group's ambitions.

'Our aim is to keep your investment low, the operation simple and to offer customers fast food that is healthier than many other products offered by other fast food restaurants,' the company says in a submission to potential franchisees. Start-up costs are low and a restaurant can be set up for as little as $65,000 in the US. Franchisees pay a fee to cover the initial training and then a royalty of 8 per cent on profits to the head office.

'Complications can hurt a franchise chain. Part of our success is due to the simplicity of the business and the ease with which it can be replicated,' says Mr DeLuca.

Copyright © The Financial Times Limited 2001. Reproduced with permission.

Questions for discussion

1   Fred DeLuca expanded Subway via franchising rather than increasing the number of corporately owned outlets. He suggests that different skills are needed to manage franchising operations, and hints at the importance of persuasion and co-operation.

- What skills do franchisees need and what skills do corporate managers need?

- Design a training programme for each of these two groups which will satisfy these skill needs.

2   If DeLuca decided to appoint an HR specialist to Head Office with a view to enhancing the HR decisions and skills of the franchisees, how would you define the role of the HR specialist, and what skills in particular would they need?

Feedback

1   *Fred DeLuca expanded Subway via franchising rather than increasing the number of corporately owned outlets. He suggests that different skills are needed to manage franchising operations, and hints at the importance of persuasion and co-operation. What skills do franchisees need and what skills do corporate managers need? Design a training programme for each of these two groups which will satisfy these skill needs.*

Corporate managers are likely to need communication skills, negotiation, influencing and persuasion skills and strategic skills.

Franchisees are likely to need HR management and staff management skills, financial skills, basic catering/catering industry skills, collaboration skills and an understanding of marketing and advertising.

Students may suggest other skills – the most important factor is that each skill need is supported by evidence relating to the nature of the job.

The range of programmes suggested by students will vary widely – the critical question is whether the activity supports the skills development in question, and that the time spent on it is proportionate with the demands of the job.

2 *If DeLuca decided to appoint an HR specialist to Head Office with a view to enhancing the HR decisions and skills of the franchisees, how would you define the role of the HR specialist, and what skills in particular would they need?*

Given the decentralised approach to the business the likely role of the HR specialist would be adviser/consultant, and the franchisees would determine how the specialist would be used. Students may debate whether the HR specialist's services are free (paid for by HO) or whether each business pays on an activity or contract basis. The most important thing is that students need to identify how the suggested HR roles support the structural demands of the organisation. In terms of content students may consider the HR/staff management demands placed on franchisees. They are likely to employ a small number of staff, perhaps part-time, depending on location, and some temporary staff. Some franchisees, however, may operate a number of outlets and hence they may manage a group of outlet managers.

Likely skills required for the HR specialist would be a good understanding of legal requirements in terms of recruitment, selection, discipline, grievance, health, safety and equality. Training skills would be appropriate, and of course consultancy skills.

These skills are only an indication. The most important thing is that students identify the needed skills in relation to the demands of the franchisees' role.

Exercise 6.2

Issue for debate

Organisations would be more commercially effective if there were less emphasis on hierarchy and authority

Pro

If an organisation is to succeed in the product marketplace it needs its people to take responsibility, show initiative, be creative, manage change and be responsive to the customer. All of these qualities are inhibited by overemphasis on hierarchy and the obedience of subordinates to the instructions of their bosses. As the Milgram experiments show, hierarchical authority produces a blind, unthinking compliance, with the subordinate concentrating almost exclusively on responding to the boss (*see* Chapter 32). The quality of what is done is measured exclusively by how close compliance is to the instruction. Autonomy releases people from that type of dependence, so that they are not only *able* to think for themselves, but *need* so to do. Their actions are guided not by the instructions from a supervisor who must be obeyed, but from the exigencies of the situation in which they are working or from a customer who must be satisfied. It is by responding to the real needs of the business that employees make an organisation effective, not by responding to instructions from the boss.

Con

Without a clear hierarchy of authority in an organisation there is no co-ordination, and without co-ordination of effort, the 'organisation' is no more than a collection of individuals and groups pursuing diverse and conflicting goals: the benefits of synergy are lost. Furthermore the needs of the customer and the dictates of financial viability have to be interpreted in the light of overall organisational policy, which can be fully comprehended only by a few members of any undertaking. It is the result of that interpretation that should guide what other members of the organisation do, so that there is a clear direction for the activities of all and a co-ordinated drive towards the achievement of set objectives. A minority of employees need autonomy and freedom from direction, but no organisation can afford to extend those conditions to the majority, who will only be effective if they carry out their duties in line with precise instructions.

Advice on debates

Debates are not usual forms of teaching, and are usually associated with bygone eras in traditional universities. They are, however, a useful way of getting students to see both sides of a question: essential in management roles!

The best format is for one member of the group to prepare a 'pro' case beforehand, while another prepares the 'con' position. Someone in the chair then allows each person to open or oppose for 5–10 minutes, so that the two sides of the argument are presented. Theoretically other members of the group speak either in favour of, or against, the motion. In practice they are more likely to raise questions or make brief comments. The main protagonists then sum up and there is a vote.

On the first occasion it is probably best for the lecturer to chair the proceedings, but on other occasions this can be done by a member of the group. Using members of staff to be the opening speakers can be a useful device, as they can be instructed to disagree sharply with each other, not pulling any punches. Everyone will like that.

The person in the chair has to make it clear that votes are for and against the motion and not for or against the personalities. It is also important that everyone at the beginning realises that they have to vote at the end, so they are working out their view as well as listening to what is being said. Permit, but do not encourage abstentions.

CHAPTER 7   COMMUNICATION AND INFORMATION

The first half of this chapter deals with communication, and in particular concentrates on communications to all employees or groups of employees, rather than one-to-one communication which is covered in more detail in other chapters (*see*, for example, those dealing with individual performance management, appraisal skills, discipline and grievance). However many of the communication principles described in this chapter apply equally to one-to-one communication.

This chapter focuses on the meaning and scope of organisational communication with an emphasis on both formal and informal channels and the importance of a two-way process. The purposes of communication are briefly reviewed and then barriers to communication are discussed in some detail. The last section on communication deals with the appropriateness of different methods of communication in different circumstances, and reports some results from the most recent WERS survey.

The second half of the chapter reviews information in organisations. A model of HR information is presented which incorporates individual employee information, aggregate employee information, information about HR systems and activities and information on the HR function. After each aspect of the model has been discussed in some detail the focus moves to the content and implications of 1998 Data Protection Act.

Additional teaching material

Two exercises are provided here to support teaching of the material in Chapter 7, looking at different aspects of organisational communication. The first is a *Financial Times* article focusing on an episode at the Dresdner Bank. The second invites students to debate the research of Tixier looking at variations in communication styles in different countries. A further suggested classroom activity is outlined at the end.

Exercise 7.1

The following case study focuses on an unusual, high-impact approach to organisational communication at the Dresdner bank. Questions for discussion and exercises based on the case follow the article. Feedback for lecturers is also provided.

INSIDE TRACK: Hearts and minds set for recovery

By Tony Major, *Financial Times*, 23 July 2001

When 16,000 Dresdner Bank staff turned up at nine conference centres and exhibition halls across Germany one Friday afternoon late last month, they had little idea of what was in store.

They had heard that the bank management might talk about strategy. Some feared news of further job losses. There were even rumours of a grand party.

In the event, the staff, from the retail and private client division, were treated to 3½ hours of intense discussion and comic-book graphics explaining the bank's 'blueprint for recovery'.

The 'get-together', which ended late in the day with food and live music, was promoted by Andreas Georgi, the 44-year-old Dresdner Bank board member responsible for the retail banking division.

Mr Georgi, who inherited a retail banking business battered and bruised by the failure of two mergers last year, was keen to reach the 'hearts and minds' of his staff to generate enthusiasm for badly needed changes at the bank. The looming takeover by Allianz, the German insurer, had given added urgency to the project.

'We had a good strategy – outlined by Bernd Fahrholz at the annual shareholders meeting in May last year – but we needed the full support of staff to implement it,' he says. Mr Fahrholz announced a plan aimed at transforming Dresdner into a 'European advisory bank' focused on the capital markets. Dresdner was to concentrate on its core businesses, solve the biggest problems in unprofitable retail banking and invest for the future. But that meant shedding 5,000 jobs and closing 300 out of 1,150 domestic branches. Employees and unions were never likely to be keen on such cost-cutting.

To win them over, Mr Fahrholz and his management team decided that staff had to understand 'the vision and goals' of the bank's recovery plan. But what would be the best way of convincing sceptical employees of the need for radical change?

Mr Georgi believed it was time for something completely different. He had spent a few days 'under cover' in some of Dresdner's branches last year. He found branch staff fearful for the future and unsettled by the lack of information filtering down to them.

He favoured an approach that produced 'maximum impact'. It could not rely on line management communicating the bank's strategy to staff. He wanted to reach everyone with one shot by creating a day they would never forget.

That is when Dresdner Bank, an institution with 120 years of history, decided to contact Root Learning, an 11-year-old Ohio-based company that specialises in change management. 'We focus on making complex business issues understandable to every employee at every level of a company,' says Donald McLean of Root Learning. 'We do it by combining strong visual images with Socratic dialogue,' he adds. 'We've worked with more than 120 companies – it works.' The idea is simple: everyone in a company must understand the overall organisation in order to get the wheels of change turning.

Root's clients have included Charles Schwab and UPS in the US and Lufthansa and Siemens Nixdorf in Germany.

At the core of Root's methodology are its 'Root Maps', comic-book-style visuals that use metaphors to explain the key issues confronting a company. 'When I saw some of the charts I did have my doubts,' says Mr Georgi. Bankers, after all, are a conservative breed. But Dresdner, eager to make a statement of commitment to staff, decided to stick with it.

The fruit of weeks of painstaking discussion was three main 'maps' that portrayed the competitive German banking market, the structure of Dresdner's retail business and the bank's future as part of the Allianz group.

The poster-size charts used cars (Dresdner was a BMW, Deutsche a Mercedes, Commerzbank a VW Lupo, the public sector savings banks a minibus), roads, bridges, rivers and icebergs to explain the bank's strategy and future prospects.

They were presented to employees in groups of 10 who, with the help of a facilitator, then discussed the content of the maps. Mr McLean says this 'Socratic style' of dialogue is 'the engine of our methodology'. People have 'to ask questions in order to develop an understanding of issues'. The aim, he says, 'is to avoid presenting conclusions' and encourage staff 'to find out for themselves through exploration and inquiry'.

Did the exercise work? Feedback so far shows that more than 80 per cent of employees found the project valuable. And Mr Georgi believes it worked. 'The reaction was great. People in the branches represent the public face of the bank. They have to be convinced of the bank's strategy – of the need for change.' He says they now are.

Questions for discussion

1   Dresdner Bank decided to discuss the new strategy with all bank employees at the same time in nine parallel sessions. What are the advantages and disadvantages of this approach compared with, say, a phased cascade through different levels of staff?

2   Dresdner Bank used visual images, cartoons and metaphors to get the message across. What the advantages and disadvantages of such an approach?

3   Using the idea of the car metaphor and a food metaphor:

  - describe your organisation using both these metaphors;

  - describe the institution where you study (if appropriate) using both these metaphors;

  - write an explanation of why you have chosen these metaphors;

  - how helpful was the metaphor approach in understanding the nature of your organisation/place of study?

4   What are the advantages and disadvantages of using the 'Socratic' approach which the bank adopted?

Feedback

1   *Dresdner Bank decided to discuss the new strategy with all bank employees at the same time in nine parallel sessions. What are the advantages and disadvantages of this approach compared with, say, a phased cascade through different levels of staff?*

Advantages that are noted are likely to include prevention of rumours, especially amongst those who are last in a communications programme; inclusiveness, as no one is left until last; inclusiveness as all levels of staff are communicated with together; aids communication and effectiveness of staff as all get the same message at the same time; speed.

Disadvantages may focus on the question of whether the same offering is appropriate for all levels of staff (senior staff vs. branch counter staff for example); may alienate senior staff; it has to be right first time as there is no allowance for feedback to be fed into a rolling communications programme.

2   *Dresdner Bank used visual images, cartoons and metaphors to get the message across. What the advantages and disadvantages of such an approach?*

Advantages may be that the message is easier to remember; it is easier to relate to message; a fun experience may result in a more positive outlook.

Disadvantages are that some may feel this method is beneath them; metaphors may be regarded as being psycho-babble; not seen as serious.

4   *What are the advantages and disadvantages of using the 'Socratic' approach which the bank adopted?*

Advantages can be seen in relation to higher levels of understanding as people have been made to think it through; increased commitment as they have been allowed to challenge things; increased commitment as they have been a part of the process.

Disadvantages may focus on the time needed; unpredictability; and the skill required of managers/facilitators.

Exercise 7.2

European variations in communication styles

Read the following summary of Tixier's work comparing and contrasting preferred communication styles in different European countries. Learning activities associated with her findings are provided at the end.

Tixier (1994) has researched management and communication styles in Europe, and while she argues that the diversity of styles is so complex that it is difficult to draw conclusions, she does identify six dimensions of communications styles. These are:

1   *Preference for either oral or written communication* – she found that the Germans, Dutch and Portuguese favoured written communication, and could not, for example, understand the high telephone bills of French subsidiaries which rely much more heavily on oral communication. She also found that verbal agreements have a different value in different countries.

2   *Length of written communication* – she argues that, partly as a result of the nature of the language and partly as a result of early conditioning, there are differences in the length of written communication considered to be appropriate in different countries. She suggests that it is difficult to be concise in French, and that for Greeks a longer communication is considered to create a more favourable impression.

3   *Implicit and explicit communication* – Tixier suggests that while some countries prefer simple and tight communications with no room for ambiguity (for example, Germany), others prefer a more subtle and suggestive approach which needs reading between the lines (France, for example).

4   *Clarity* – this is linked to the dimension above, and relates to the degree of precision required. For example, the British and Swedes allow more room for individual initiative in responding to a communication.

5   *Formality* – Tixier suggests that such countries as Italy, Portugal, Germany and Austria prefer a more formal style of address (as in the formal version of 'you', and the use of titles), whereas in Ireland, Luxembourg, Switzerland and the Scandinavian countries a less formal approach is preferred. She associates these differences partly with the importance of symbols of power and recognition in different countries and the extent to which the culture is 'egalitarian'.

6   *More or less direct modes of communication* – related to the above, Tixier suggests that preferences in directness are expressed in both written and oral communication: for example, the acceptability of criticism and overt conflict. She suggests the Nordics are very careful about how criticism is expressed, whereas in Spain and Italy it is acceptable to have a more 'noisy and scathing' approach.

Summarised from: Tixier, M. (1994) 'Management and communication styles in Europe: can they be compared and matched?', *Employee Relations*, Vol. 16, No. 1, pp. 8–26.

Associated student activities

1   Think of your own organisation and consider the culture of communication in your organisation. What methods and approaches are important and accepted, and what methods and approaches are less acceptable? What is the impact of this on the way that the organisation works?

2   Write down your own personal preferences in terms of communication. Now compare these with the preferences of your managers and those of your subordinates (if you have any). What is the impact of these styles on the way you work together?

Feedback

There are no guideline answers, but if this is used as a student activity you may also wish to question:

- The extent to which communications cultures vary within the organisation .

- Whether some people fail to come to terms with the communications culture.

- The problems caused when two people have a different communications style.

- Whether individuals deliberately match their personal communications style to that of their boss/subordinates.

Further activity

Develop some current and critical methods of organisational communication (e.g. team briefing, focus groups) by asking two or three students to make a 10-minute presentation (prepared in advance) of how one of these methods works in their organisation or one with which they are familiar.

Allow time for questions and discussion of other students' experiences after each presentation, and explore further by using the following framework:

- In which direction is the communication?
- For whose benefit is the communication?
- How effective is this method in theory?
- How effective is this method in practice?

CHAPTER 8 INTERACTIVE SKILL: CHAIRING MEETINGS

In this chapter (new to the fifth edition) we consider how to run a meeting, and to some extent how to take part in a meeting which you do not chair.

In terms of teaching, much will depend on what experience of meetings the members of the group have. For this reason it may be best to start with Activity 8.1, as this will gradually tease out meetings that people do not immediately think of, like meeting to choose the hockey captain at school, or even a family arguing about where to go on holiday. It also enables those with less experience to learn from those with more.

Then the material on meeting preparation needs to be presented to the whole group before the first exercise is run. The methods are described in the chapter, but it can be useful to monitor the later stages of the discussion. Among the more common shortcomings found in groups using this exercise are the following:

- The brief or terms of reference being too general and/or too broad, going beyond what the group can usefully consider.

- Too little attention being given to the sequence of items on the agenda.

- Difficulty in deciding what the meeting is for.

The three suggestions in the chapter are not the only possibilities. The two topics suggested would require a combination of sharing information and making a decision.

If the suggested topics are not suitable, other possibilities could be:

- What lies ahead of HRM as the next development phase for personnel professionals?

- What are the advantages and drawbacks of downsizing or delayering to the employees of a business?

After the material on the encounter has been presented, the second exercise could then be run, with the lecturer taking part in the final discussion to make sure that participants concentrate on their own individual learning, as people will take quite different things from it. Few will 'do well' in chairing, so it is important to focus on individual learning, rather than applauding one or more good performances.

A useful way of winding up the session is to ask the whole group to call out ideas for Activity 8.2.

Here are the two short, practical role play exercises on chairing meetings included on the student-side of this website.

Exercise in meeting preparation

You need a small group of 5–8, ideally of fellow students, who have a shared interest in a topic like organising the course Christmas party, or making suggestions about how the course should be organised next year.

- Agree who is to chair the meeting and who is to take notes.

- Follow the check questions in the section of the chapter on preparation.

- Discuss the notes that have been prepared and agree the agenda.

Exercise in the conduct of meetings

Change the person chairing the meeting and start working through the agenda, following the section of the chapter describing the encounter. Everybody else takes part in the discussion in as normal a way as possible: no sabotage!

After 10–15 minutes, switch to a different person in the chair and continue.

At the close of the meeting, discuss the experience by considering the following:

- Reactions of the two chairs to their experience in running the meeting.

- Comments by other participants on what the chairs have said.

- Comments by other participants on their experience in taking part in the meeting, with constructive comments on how they responded to the two styles of leadership.

- General discussion on the effectiveness of the meeting.

PART II CASE STUDY FEEDBACK

In June 1997, Incomes Data Services calculated that there were 250,000 people working in call centres, with the number set to rise as more and more use is made of the call centre system. Employees are predominantly women, with a key salary range of £9,500 to £11,500. At least half the people employed are on full-time contracts, and that proportion can rise to 70 per cent or even 80 per cent in some centres.

Tentative approaches to the six questions are:

1, 2 and **3**:   There need to be 120 operators available between 08.00 and 22.00 (14 hours); 80 between 10.00 and 17.00 (7 hours); 230 from 17.00 to 21.00 (4 hours). This staffing level is needed seven days a week. That can be calculated as:

$$120 \times 14 \times 7 = 11,760$$
$$80 \times 7 \times 7 = 3,920$$
$$230 \times 4 \times 7 = 6,440$$

Total: 22,120 operator hours

From that basis the discussion begins on how many will be full-time and part-time, how the hours will be organised, and so forth. There will probably be a basic day shift from 08.00 to 17.00, with full-time staff working four shifts a week. A second day shift could run from 10.00 to 19.00, with part-timers working evenings. The discussion will, however, range over other matters, such as the feasibility of people working as flexibly as the operating hours will require, and whether there will need to be heavy part-time cover at weekends, together with all the other practical problems that are involved.

4   It is basically a bureaucratic structure with a flat hierarchy. It has to be bureaucratic because of the need for absolute consistency in what is said to the customer. There can be scope for wide variations of individual style, but the substance of what is said has to be consistent. There are usually working teams of 12–15, with a supervisor or team leader, forming the basic operational unit.

5   Obviously the easiest form of communication is the screen in front of the operator, which can display most of the information that the operator needs, but training and briefing sessions away from the screens are a regular feature, especially when there are regular changes of product lines or pricing arrangements.

6   The method adopted seem to be twofold: the office layout and the pay scheme. The working area is open plan with a very lively, 'chatty' atmosphere encouraged, so that there is maximum scope for interpersonal chat and badinage in the lulls between calls. Pay arrangements typically include a proportion of bonus or incentive payments, linked to targets. The targets are set not only to meet the needs of the organisation but also to stimulate the working teams. They are often dreamed up by the team leader, with one set for a particular week, but then abandoned in favour of a different, novel idea. Achievements of targets are usually celebrated by a trip to the pub at the close of the shift.

No doubt your students will have better ideas.

CHAPTER 9 STRATEGIC ASPECTS OF RESOURCING

In this chapter we introduce the central themes to be covered in the other chapters on employee resourcing. The main focus is on labour markets and the need for organisations to understand their dynamics in order to develop strategies for competing in them. We present several tools for analysing labour markets, while also looking at different forms of flexibility. Recent debates about the rights and wrongs of flexibility are also assessed.

Additional teaching material

The following news article published in the *Financial Times* in May 2001 illustrates many of the issues and management choices discussed in Chapter 9. It also provides a useful starting point for discussion about recruitment and retention in the healthcare sector generally – an important and very topical political issue about which students should find it straightforward to articulate a view. Suggested discussion questions, together with some feedback, are presented below.

NHS spends £1bn a year on temps

By Nicholas Timmins, *Financial Times*, 15 May 2001

The National Health Service is spending £1bn a year on temporary, agency and locum staff, according to a study by the healthcare analysts Laing and Buisson.

Demand for agency staff is rising across the private as well as the public healthcare sector amid chronic staff shortages in virtually all healthcare occupations, according to the report.

The size of the market for agency staff has more than quadrupled since 1992, with the NHS almost trebling its spend over a similar period. However, home nursing, home helps and other home care services at £1,125m make up the largest sector of the £2.4bn market.

Rising concern at the cost of agency staff, and worries that temporary staff provide less effective care, have led to a number of NHS initiatives to reduce their use. The NHS has created 'bank staff' and other alternatives, and is attempting to use its purchasing power to get better deals from agencies.

But 'an underlying shift towards more flexible work patterns and tight labour market conditions in the economy has driven demand for flexible staffing solutions', said Philip Blackburn, the report's author.

In addition, new entitlements to paid holiday for temporary staff have made temporary work more attractive.

'Because of training time-lags, shortages of nurses and other healthcare professionals will be a continuing feature of the British healthcare scene for several years to come,' he said.

Some of the rise is cyclical and due to low unemployment. 'Under full employment, nurses and other relatively low-paid staff benefit from an expanded choice of employment opportunities inside and outside the healthcare sector', the report says. As labour markets tighten, 'bureaux bid up the price for scarce workers and workers themselves are incentivised to switch from permanent employment to benefit from higher hourly rates as well as opportunities for more flexible hours of employment'.

Despite buoyant demand, the industry's profitability is modest, the report says. In 1999 it is estimated to have generated only £20m–£25m of pre-tax operating profit, or about 1% of turnover, and last year may have risen to about 2%. As a result, 'the NHS may be getting a better deal from agency staff providers than many critics believe', Mr Blackburn said.

The industry remains highly fragmented, with Nestor Healthcare holding about 15% of the market, Match Group holding just under 6% and no one else having more than about 3%.

There is, however, a trend towards consolidation, some of it driven by NHS Trusts looking for larger organisations with which they can negotiate competitive contracts.

www.laingbuisson.co.uk

Copyright © The Financial Times Limited 2001. Reproduced with permission.

Questions for discussion

1   Make a list of the different factors which have contributed to the growth of healthcare temping agencies in recent years.

2   Using the various models and analytical tools presented in Chapter 9:

(a)   Analyse the labour market described in the article.

(b)   Identify the major strategic choices made by NHS managers in interacting with the labour market.

3   What long-term labour market developments are necessary in order for skills shortages in nursing and other healthcare professions to ease?

Feedback

1   *Make a list of the different factors which have contributed to the growth of healthcare temping agencies in recent years.*

- Increased demand for healthcare workers in both private and public sectors (ageing population, more medical interventions available, etc.).

- Tight labour market conditions/low unemployment, giving healthcare workers alternative job opportunities.

- Too few trained nurses and doctors (supply insufficient to meet demand) gives agencies a role in helping employers plug gaps.

- Better conditions for temporary staff (paid holidays now provided plus good rates of pay).

- Staff shortages mean that temping in healthcare is a reasonably 'secure' job.

- Attractiveness of temping to workers who value independence, flexibility, variety, etc.

2   *Using the various models and analytical tools presented in Chapter 9:*

(a)   *Analyse the labour market described in the article.*

- *Geography* – this is now an international market. Healthcare workers are routinely recruited from overseas to work in the NHS.

- *Tight vs. loose* – clearly very tight.

- *Occupational structure* – very much a craft structure.

- *Generational* – crosses the generations, few Nexters (born since 1980) in this labour market as yet.

- *Numerical flexibility* – temping agencies, by their nature, support organisations needing numerical flexibility (i.e. subject to fluctuating demand for staff).

- *Temporal flexibility* – less relevant here, as healthcare organisations need staffing round the clock via shift systems. Demand for staff does not fluctuate at short notice during the day except where there is a lot of short-term absenteeism.

- *Functional flexibility* – jobs in healthcare tend to be specialised and quite narrowly defined, though there have been some moves towards functional flexibility in recent years with the growth of 'health care assistants' trained to carry out a variety of support activities.

- *Sonnenfield model* – healthcare has traditionally most closely resembled the 'club' form. This article demonstrates a shift towards the 'baseball team'.

(b)   *Identify the major strategic choices made by NHS managers in interacting with the labour market.*

When labour markets tighten, employers can take a number of approaches:

(i)   Work harder at recruiting.

(ii)   Recruit outside their customary labour market.

(iii)   Improve terms and conditions to attract and retain more staff.

(iv)   Seek to make jobs more interesting, enjoyable, etc.

(v)   Improve the working environment.

(vi)   Reduce their reliance on hard-to-recruit groups.

NHS managers have sought to do all of these to a greater or lesser extent, but have been restricted by ever-present budgetary constraints. Most of the activity has thus focused on (ii) and (vi) which are the least costly and quickest strategies. There has been extensive overseas recruitment and also attempts made to persuade trained staff working in other areas to return to the NHS. Reorganisations and skill-mix reviews have been the main methods used to reduce the need for scarce and highly qualified staff, together with initiatives such as NHS Direct which seeks to replace a doctor's appointments with a 24-hour helpline.

3   *What long-term labour market developments are necessary in order for skills shortages in nursing and other healthcare professions to ease?*

- Increased supply (more trained personnel available).

- Decreased demand (further reorganisations, etc.).

- Reduced opportunities for staff to take other jobs (i.e. a recession would be helpful).

- Improved terms and conditions.

Topics for debate

The following topics, directly related to the material in Chapter 9, are suitable for classroom debate or as the basis of assignment questions.

1   *The strategy of internal recruitment is more likely than external recruitment to produce continuing effectiveness in organisational performance*

Pro

Promotion from within rewards those who have contributed well to business objectives and therefore reinforces those behaviours and attitudes. Those promoted to senior posts have a deep understanding of the business and how its organisation works. They will be fully versed in all the cultural subtleties and will not have a steep learning curve to climb. Loyalty is seen to pay off and newcomers will believe that they have genuine career prospects by staying with the business rather than exploiting their opportunities and moving on.

Con

Promotion from within is a dangerous practice, as it reinforces methods and attitudes that have been successful in the past. Perhaps those approaches are exactly what is needed for the foreseeable future, but there is likely to be complacency and self-satisfaction. Recruiting externally means there is constant challenge to assumptions about values, culture and method. Also those who are developing their careers within the business are kept on their toes, so that there will be a continuing openness to new ideas and opportunities.

2 *Increasing employee flexibility is incompatible with increasing employee loyalty*

Pro

Flexibility weakens the bonds of mutual loyalty between employer and individual employees. The time horizon is shorter in the case of temporary staff. The amount of time spent at work is less in the case of part-time work, making the workplace less central to the employee's life. Those working on a subcontracted/self-employed basis are, by the nature of their contractual relationship, less loyal. They may work for other employers at the same time and will want to maintain contacts outside the organisation for which they are currently working so as to secure future work. Peripheral workers are often seen as being more disposable (as in the flexible firm model) and will perceive themselves as such. The whole basis of the psychological contract is thus different from that of full-time permanent staff.

Con

Just because someone works on an atypical contract it does not necessarily mean that that person will be less loyal. They may well see their employment, for example on a fixed-term basis, as a precursor to future permanent employment. They are just as likely to form close working relationships with colleagues as are full-time, permanent staff and may enjoy the work more *because* it is less central to their lives. Part-time staff are often very long-serving employees, who stay because of the flexibility their hours give them. They often have considerably more organisational knowledge than relative newcomers working full-time and may have fewer alternative career options as a result. Ultimately much depends on how people are managed. Organisations can attract immense loyalty from employees very early on in their mutual relationship provided they treat them well and provide them with a satisfying place of work.

CHAPTER 10 CONTRACTS, CONTRACTORS AND CONSULTANTS

Different forms of contractual relationship, introduced in Chapter 9, take centre stage in Chapter 10. We start by defining the contract of employment in legal terms, stating what its significance is in terms of accruable employment rights. We move on to look in some detail at different types of contract and at different patterns of working. We focus on part-time, temporary and distance working, as well as on different examples of subcontracting. The final part of the chapter looks at the employment of consultants, with a particular focus on their use on HR projects.

Additional teaching material

The following two articles, both taken from the *Financial Times* (FT.com) website, offer rather different assessments of teleworking, a form of contractual or working arrangement that many believe will become increasingly common. The topic is introduced towards the end of Chapter 10. These articles look at it in greater detail. Suggested discussion questions and feedback are provided at the end.

Article 10.1

New direction – freelancing means independence, but with a catch

By Sarah Murray, FT.com website, 20 August 2001

It seems like a dream – working without meetings, bosses, office politics, dress codes or employee appraisals, where your time is your own and where you can take a holiday whenever it suits you. And plenty of formerly salaried employees agree – one in four Americans is now employed as a freelancer. But giving up the job and going it alone is not something upon which to embark lightly.

First, before the money can start to roll in, there's the question of your office infrastructure. As a journalist, mine seemed relatively simple – a phone, a laptop computer, an e-mail address and an internet connection. Stationery was also a consideration and I had business cards designed and printed. But in a world where e-mail rules, expensive stationery and fax paper are hardly a necessity. Indeed, my needs seemed minimal – a desk and a chair completed the picture and I was ready to go.

That was until, my new computer crashed. Faced with a blank screen and a five o'clock deadline, life as a free agent suddenly seemed a little more perilous than I'd anticipated. And when it transpired that the help line I'd been given by the company that made my computer was permanently busy, things started to look bleak.

Leaving a large company to work from home, it is easy to forget just how much is provided on site. Everything from the light bulbs and postal collections to the ergonomic furniture and the computer system is supplied and maintained by somebody else. When you have computer problems at the office, you can always call up a technician, and if they can't fix it, they find you another one. Secretaries and assistants are on hand to organise packages that need couriering and heating and air-conditioning are freely available.

Vivien Wang, an architect who recently left a Manhattan practice to go freelance, says she had not realised how much equipment she would need to install in order to get her practice up and running. 'I only have one phone line and that's servicing my phone, fax and internet,' she says. 'I don't have a photocopier – a lot of time I have to enlarge and reduce drawings – and all my files are set up for the office printer so I've had to reconfigure them.'

Nevertheless, surviving outside the office environment is far easier than it would have been 10 or 20 years ago. Most people now do their own typing, voicemail takes messages and e-mail cuts out the need to use the postal system as frequently. Documents that once had to be printed out and couriered round to another office can now be sent as e-mail attachments. The availability of information over the internet has also made freelance work possible for those who need to conduct extensive research.

And the costs associated with working from home have dropped dramatically. While fuel and electricity bills rise once you are spending your working day at home, judicious use of e-mail can keep the phone bills at a manageable level.

Even those whose profession involves using larger machinery find solutions are on hand. Markus Hodapp, a London-based landscape gardener, did not invest heavily in equipment when he set up his business. 'I had a van, but not a digger or a compressor,' he says. 'You only need to use these things every so often – and it's very easy to hire all that stuff now.'

Being a free agent can also have substantial tax advantages. In the US for example, freelancers can offset a wide range of items against their tax bill. For those using the home as an office, deductions include mortgage interest or rent payments, insurance, repairs and maintenance and utilities bills. Other deductions include such things as professional fees, stationery, travel and a portion of entertainment costs and advertising expenses.

Even pitching for work has become easier, with the recent proliferation of websites matching freelancers with contracts, such as freeagent.com, smarterwork.com, guru.com and elance.com.
But as well as changing the light bulbs and fixing the computers, big companies provide something far more important – work-related benefits. Items such as membership of the local gym, health insurance and a pension plan boost the real value of a salaried job substantially and can be costly when you have to finance them yourself.

Employers also provide something of great importance – space. 'At the moment, I'm going a little crazy because my work and life are all in the same apartment,' says Ms Wang. 'When I was building a model for clients in New Jersey recently, I had the parts all over the floor and I couldn't move. So it's figuring out how to work and live in the same place.'

But despite all the hassles, freelancers – myself included – frequently cite the sense of freedom as the main benefit of working independently. While it often means putting in longer hours than office workers who can walk away at the end of the day, the feeling that your time is your own is a compelling reason for going it alone.

'You may not have a boss – but in fact you have a much bigger boss: yourself,' says Mr Hodapp.

'So even though I work harder than I would do if I worked for somebody else, I don't mind because it's for me.'

Ms Wang says that, in addition to this, she experiences more creative freedom than she did as an employee. 'The projects are now my projects and it gives me more design freedom,' she says. 'I'm doing stuff that I would never have considered before because of the constraints of the way my company worked – I've felt so liberated.'

Copyright © The Financial Times Group 2001. Reproduced with permission.

Article 10.2:

NATIONAL NEWS: Telework revolution failing to catch on, says TUC

By Nicholas Timmins, *Financial Times*, 4 August 2001

Predictions that teleworking – working at home with a computer – will lead to a revolution in office work have failed to materialise, a report from the Trades Union Congress concluded yesterday.

Instead, home computers are more likely to be used by stressed executives taking work home at the weekend, or by the kind of worker, usually self-employed, who has always worked from home.

Teleworking is increasing – up by 40 per cent between 1998 and 2000 – and can offer employees greater choice and flexibility and improve the work–life balance, the report says. It is likely to increase: 'But it is not driving a fundamental shift in work organisation or the balance between working at home and working in office.'

The report defines telework to include those whose main job is at home with use of a telephone and computer as a key part of that; those who work in different places but use their home as a base; and 'occasional' teleworkers who do so at least one day a week.

In spring last year, the report estimates nearly 1.6m people, or nearly 6 per cent of the workforce, fell into one of those categories. But only about 130,000, half a per cent, were working full-time at home rather than in a factory or office. Those who did so only occasionally were far more common.

The report says that in the 1990s there appeared to have been an overall decline in home-working, despite the rise of the teleworkers. 'The balance in the location of work between office and home is not changing significantly. Most forms of telework are essentially old wine in new bottles, albeit enhanced and improved by the use of computers.'

For the vast majority of manual and less skilled non-manual jobs, teleworking is not an option. Some such jobs – data entry, copytaking and coding questionnaires – can be as open to abuse as traditional forms of low-paid home working. And even for well-paid professionals it can lead to social isolation, stress and over-long hours, the report says.

It acknowledges, however, that teleworking can bring significant gains and transform the image of home-working. It can also help mothers with young children maintain a link to the labour market.

Telework – the New Industrial Revolution, www.tuc.org.uk.

Copyright © The Financial Times Limited 2001. Reproduced with permission.

Questions for discussion

1   Think about five or six jobs with which you are familiar. They may be jobs that you have held yourself, or those held by friends and family. For each, write down the major job duties. Then work out how much of the job could realistically be carried out from home on a tele-working basis. Could any be realistically carried out on a subcontracted or freelance basis?

2   What would need to change in terms of job design, equipment and conditions of employment to enable the jobs to be carried out wholly or partly from home on either an employed or a freelance basis?

Feedback

1   *Think about five or six jobs with which you are familiar. They may be jobs that you have held yourself, or those held by friends and family. For each, write down the major job duties. Then work out how much of the job could realistically be carried out from home on a tele-working basis. Could any be realistically carried out on a subcontracted or freelance basis?*

Answers here will clearly vary depending on the job chosen. The following conditions are usually necessary for a job to be carried out on a teleworking basis:

- No daily face-to-face customer role.

- No daily meetings necessary with others.

- No equipment required which can not be set up in the home.

- No need for close supervision.

2   *What would need to change in terms of job design, equipment and conditions of employment to enable the jobs to be carried out wholly or partly from home on either an employed or a freelance basis?*

Examples are as follows:

- Organise meetings for one day of the week.

53

- Make information available via an intranet that can be accessed from home.

- Videoconferencing facilities.

- Job duties phrased to focus on outputs rather than on presence at a place of work.

- Cultural change – less supervision, more trust, etc.

CHAPTER 11 RECRUITMENT

This chapter takes the reader through the main phases of a recruitment episode or campaign from determining the vacancy to shortlisting for interview. The main focus, however, is on the major alternative recruitment methods and the advantages and disadvantages of each. The most lengthy sections cover recruitment advertising and the relatively recent evolution of e-recruitment via the internet.

Additional teaching material

The following article addresses one of the most fundamental issues in the field of staff recruitment: the extent to which the employer should 'sell the job' by stressing only its positive aspects. The case study company cited in the article takes a very contrary view, advocating the use of realistic and negative messages as well as those which are positive. The discussion questions at the end should provide a vehicle for the clarification of thinking about these issues.

INSIDE TRACK: Warts-and-all hiring policy. The way to attract the right staff is to tell them the truth, says Jim Pickard

By Jim Pickard, *Financial Times*, 28 August 2001

Recruitment professionals are rarely shy of over-promotion when it comes to job descriptions. To call a spade a spade is anathema to many. A shop assistant is a 'sales consultant' and a dustman is a 'waste professional'.

Applicants for some of the dullest jobs are told that they are entering a new life of thrills and endless fun. Jobs come with the promise of fast-track promotion and career prospects, even if this is patently untrue, and many people are promised plenty of responsibility.

Graduate trainees are often interviewed at plush hotels where they are seduced with expensive food and given recruitment brochures whose glossy images do not match the reality of managing cantankerous workers at a Midlands food factory. Behind the marble statues and glorious fountains in the reception foyer of many large corporations, there are the back offices, check-outs and dank kitchens where people do the real work.

Such practices do not translate into a successful recruitment policy, according to Kaisen, a business psychologist firm dedicated to debunking some conventional wisdom.

If an employer pretends a job is more exciting than it is, recruits will soon feel let down once they notice the gap between the fiction and the reality. And they will leave.

In the call centre industry, where recruiters search for dynamic extraverts – who then spend day after day processing routine inquiries – the turnover of staff is notorious. 'Churn rates', as they are called, are higher than in most other industries. The price of this is more than just the cost of recruiting a new member of staff; when the cost of training, advertising and time lost are taken into account, it can add up to three times the employee's annual salary, according to some estimates.

Kaisen, based in Bristol, shares its expertise with the likes of Royal and Sun Alliance, Boots and Pearson, the *Financial Times*'s parent company. Kaisen is no fan of recruitment agencies. They can be a poor way of finding new staff because they often receive commissions for every person they place, says director Gwyn Rogers. 'Agencies can sometimes be undiscriminating, which leaves the onus on the individual organisation to screen people. These agencies do not always filter people out properly.'

One of Kaisen's mantras is that recruiters should give applicants the whole story, 'warts and all'. If the job is repetitive and mundane, tell the applicants. If there is little freedom for independent thought, spell it out. If people's chances of promotion are strictly limited, do not pretend otherwise. To do so would only be to store up trouble for the future.

For there are people – and these are the ones you want to employ – who in fact enjoy the security and comfort that such a job may offer.

Each person's motivation differs from the next. It is vital to match that motivation with his or her career, says Robert Myatt, a Kaisen consultant: 'Companies tend to focus on skills, not on motivation. A person could have all the skills in the world but if they are not motivated, and do not find the job interesting, they will be no good.'

For several clients, including retailers and call centre companies, Kaisen has made promotional videos that are almost brutal in their honesty. Played by actors, the videos feature 'workers' from the companies concerned, talking about their typical day and what they like or dislike about their work. They may moan about frustrating customers, or awkward colleagues, or the sheer monotony of their job. Often they talk about the late hours they have to work.

After the applicants have watched the videos, they talk to the interviewer about what struck them particularly. From this, it is often easy to spot who would be unsuitable.

A typical video may have a 'worker' chatting away. Her first sentence may be: 'The only thing I love about working here is there is a clear set of procedures: you always know the way things should be done.' The second sentence has a catch to it: 'Of course, there are lots of opportunities to move on: I don't have to do the same thing again and again.'

If the applicant is inspired by the second sentence, he or she is unlikely to be suitable for the repetitive work of a call centre.

The feedback can be interesting, says Mr Myatt: 'We have had people who have watched the video and they talk about the job and say they like the idea that they can move on, that there is light at the end of the tunnel. They see it as a step to another career, rather than being excited about the job itself.' If so, they are probably not right for the job.

Sometimes videos are used but other methods include audio cassettes and written material. All are deployed to the same effect. Mr Rogers says it is all about trust between the employer and the employee. Honesty is the best policy.

'If you see an advert for television air time sales, you may think: "TV – that is creative and exciting and open-ended. I'll get to meet the stars." In reality, you will end up in an office block in London with no windows, trying to sell to agencies,' he says.

Boots Wellbeing has recently been recruiting health and beauty professionals and others from the medical arena, such as osteopaths and nutritionists, who tend to work alone. It was vital to find those who could work in a large corporation and could handle all the necessary compromises. 'Quite rare beasts', according to Kaisen.

By eliminating unsuitable people early, Kaisen believes, it can save its clients money. Just as important is the effect on morale, it argues. 'Often people say they were surprised at how honest the company was about what the job was like,' says Mr Rogers. This, he says, leads them to regard the company positively.

Copyright © The Financial Times Limited 2001. Reproduced with permission.

Questions for discussion

1   To what extent do you agree with the approach to recruitment described in the article?

2   What are its main disadvantages?

3   The companies cited in the article use videos and other materials which carry a realistic message at the selection stage as a means of helping them and the candidates to establish their suitability for the jobs concerned. Is there also an argument for putting out 'warts and all' messages in recruitment advertisements, at graduate recruitment presentations or in notices placed at job centres?

Feedback

1   *To what extent do you agree with the approach to recruitment described in the article?*

Arguments for are:

- Realistic job preview ensures only the genuinely committed will take the job.

- Less danger of unreal expectations of a job being built up and dashed.

- Honesty and openness leads to productive and high-trust relationships at work.

2   *What are its main disadvantages?*

- May mean that good potential employees are put off from applying or accepting a job.

- Reduces ability to compete for staff when other employers are being more exclusively positive.

- May demoralise new employees when managers want them to come in bounding with enthusiasm.

- May make managers complacent about improving the work environment in order to compete more effectively for staff.

3   *The companies cited in the article use videos and other materials which carry a realistic message at the selection stage as a means of helping them and the candidates to establish their suitability for the jobs concerned. Is there also an argument for putting out 'warts and all' messages in recruitment advertisements, at graduate recruitment presentations or in notices placed at job centres?*

- The same arguments apply: there is a need to balance the potential advantages outlined above with the danger of failing to compete as effectively as rivals in the search for good employees.

- The best case can be made in organisations that are faced with very large (i.e. unmanageable) numbers of applicants; a warts and all recruitment ad may well help to reduce the number of applications from unsuitable or uncommitted job-seekers

Further suggested exercise

Run a co-ordinated group project, using up to four small groups to carry out an assignment before the session and present the results to the rest. The assignment is for each group to analyse recruitment advertisements for a different (specified) type of post, so that the advertising approach for the different jobs can be compared. The basis for the analysis could be the points under the heading **Drafting the advertisement** in the chapter, together with an assessment of cost and reach. The types of job to be analysed will depend on the make up of the group, but possibilities include:

- Chief Executive
- Financial Controller
- Personal Assistant/Private Secretary
- HGV driver
- HR/Personnel Officer

CHAPTER 12 SELECTION METHODS AND DECISIONS

The emphasis in this chapter is on selection as a two-way process rather than an aspect of managerial prerogative. We briefly consider the role of the HR specialist in selection and have found that specialists remain involved in spite of moves towards the devolution of HR activities to line managers. After this we review the more traditional material on person specifications, and note the move towards fit with the organisation and its culture rather than specific fit with the job that is being applied for. We also note the incorporation of competencies into selection criteria. The middle part of the chapter recounts the standard selection devices including application forms, CVs, biodata, telephone screening, testing, portfolios, references, self-assessment, group selection methods and assessment centres. The final part of the chapter is concerned with selection decision making. Information relating to the legislation which affects the selection process is found in Chapter 21.

Additional teaching material

The following article taken from the *Financial Times CareerPoint* web pages focuses on the thorny issue of deception in employee selection. In particular, it looks at the issues surrounding the embellishing of CVs, drawing on the results of a survey which suggests that many CVs are inaccurate in important respects. Clearly this raises important questions for HR professionals. Students are invited to consider these in the questions at the end. Lecturer feedback is provided below.

Lies, damned lies and creative CVs

By Richard Donkin, FT.com CareerPoint, 10 August 2001

There has been plenty of hand-wringing in the past week about curricula vitae – or resumés, depending on which side of the Atlantic you work – and the ease with which they can be manipulated or falsified.

These self-created documents that list our working history and education can range from a brief description of achievements, work periods and dates to stylised texts delivered with the eloquence of the Gettysburg address. Some are distinguished by their brevity, with missing links or vague entries. It seems many of us take liberties with our CVs. One in three job-seekers has told lies on their CV, according to a Mori poll of 1,000 UK employees published this week by cvvalidation.com, a CV vetting company. This is because many people believe, quite rightly, that career details are rarely checked and some cannot resist the temptation of adding a qualification here or improving a university degree there.

But is it a crime? Jeff Grout, European divisional director of Robert Half International, writes in his forthcoming book *Kick Start Your Career* that 'while no recruiter would advocate lying on a CV, if you tried a job for three months, realised it was a mistake and quickly moved to something else, it might be simpler to leave it out. This is particularly true if the experience occurred some years ago and is irrelevant for your current job application.'

Economy with the truth

Mr Grout believes that the one-in-three statistic is short of the mark if it includes exaggerations: 'I think all of us to a certain extent lie by omission and create some statements that might be regarded as being economical with the truth.' A few embellishments may be acceptable but where do you draw the line? And when does an omission become a cause for alarm and investigation?

The debate has reached sanctimonious levels in the US following revelations in *The New York Times* that headhunters who recommended 'Chainsaw' Al Dunlap for top jobs in US industry, including his last post as the chairman of Sunbeam, had failed to turn up significant blemishes on his career record.

Mr Dunlap is defending a civil action brought by the Securities and Exchange Commission alleging that he and other executives cooked the books at Sunbeam to inflate its share price. He has denied any wrongdoing. The *New York Times* report revealed that this was not the first time Mr Dunlap had been investigated in connection with allegations of accounting fraud.

But neither Korn/Ferry International, the headhunters that brought him to Sunbeam, nor Spencer Stuart, who placed him in his previous job at Scott Paper, had noticed that he had been fired on two occasions – in 1973 from Max Phillips & Son and later, in 1976, from Nitec Paper, a paper milling company at Niagara Falls. The Nitec case involved similar accusations of financial manipulation that never came to trial.

Not actively concealed

Why did the headhunters not spot the missing links? The answer, apparently, is that Mr Dunlap chose not to point them out, although his lawyer has said they were never actively concealed. In a statement to *Executive Recruiter News*, an executive search industry newsletter, Korn/Ferry has stated that the decision to recruit Mr Dunlap at Sunbeam had been based 'primarily on his documented accomplishments' during the previous decade. Spencer Stuart, nearer to the missing links since they conducted the earlier search, told ERN that Mr Dunlap had made no reference to holding either of the jobs from which he was fired in the mid-1970s. James Kennedy, founder of ERN, has criticised the failure to trace Mr Dunlap's career. 'Ground zero is the place where you start,' he says. But Mr Kennedy should know, and almost every headhunter must know, that such thoroughness is rare. For most top executive appointments, as Spencer Stuart explained, prepared CVs are rarely consulted. A candidate's employment history is established during interviews. It is as if in the rarefied world of senior executive recruitment the CV is for minions, not for top people who have already proved themselves.

Establishing the merit of such accomplishments tends to engage headhunters. As Peter Felix, president of the New York-based Association of Executive Recruiters, says: 'Typically, with senior executive appointments the reference-checking concerns abilities and skills and competences and trying to get a handle on a candidate's suitability to do the job.' In the re-engineering-obsessed days of the 1980s and early 1990s when Mr Dunlap made his reputation, there seemed little doubt about his determination to get tough when he walked into a company. His reputation was based on ruthless job-cutting, not financial manipulation. Dealers who traded in stocks and shares loved what they saw and gave him the macho 'Chainsaw' nickname just as they hailed 'Neutron' Jack Welch for shedding 100,000 jobs within five years of his 1981 appointment at General Electric.

Mr Welch was able to transform his reputation into that of a builder but Mr Dunlap remained the unrepentant hacker. At Scott Paper he had laid off a third of the workforce within a year and earned himself almost $100m in salary and stock profits when he sold the company to Kimberly-Clark, its closest rival. The sale price of $6.8bn returned a 225 per cent profit on their investment to Scott Paper shareholders. These were the career statistics that mattered when Mr Dunlap became chairman of Sunbeam. On the day he joined the company, Sunbeam's stock rose 49 per cent.

References from the horse's mouth

So should the headhunters have been more diligent? The AESC has been sufficiently concerned to launch a review of search practices. Mr Felix believes it will be necessary for search firms to make clear to their clients that vetting is a specialist job. 'Search firms are not set up as private investigators. I think we have to be clear about that. We need to define who expects whom to do what. It would be ridiculous if only the search firms took references, because the hiring company must hear some of these references from the horse's mouth.'

It might make sense for the recruitment industry internationally to insist that their clients expect all job candidates, irrespective of status or position, to submit a personally prepared CV to recruiters when they are approached. Some US recruiters have been talking about 'truth in hiring statements' but these seem to be nothing more than liability waivers designed to absolve headhunters from the sin of ignorance.

For senior appointments, the CV might even become a semi-legal document to be filed with regulators. That would need legislation but it might lead people to feel less tempted to be cavalier with their declarations. In the meantime it would be good to have a single, internationally accepted name for the CV. Personally, I prefer curriculum vitae, meaning, literally, the course of one's life. It never does run smoothly.

Kick Start Your Career by Jeff Grout. To be published in the UK by John Wiley, January 2002, price £9.99.

Other recruitment stories and statistics can be viewed at FTCareerPoint.com.

Contact Richard Donkin.

Copyright © FT CareerPoint 2001. Reproduced with permission.

Questions for discussion

1   What mechanisms can HR specialists and line managers employ to check the validity of information on CVs? In what circumstances, if ever, should significant checks be made and why?

2   Application forms can sometimes elicit better information than CVs as they pose some direct questions that the CV may otherwise not address. However CVs remain highly popular. What advantages are there in using CVs for both the potential employee and the potential employer?

Feedback:

1   *What mechanisms can HR specialists and line managers employ to check the validity of information on CVs? In what circumstances, if ever, should significant checks be made and why?*

Students may suggest requesting copies of qualification certificates and checking with awarding bodies in order to confirm qualifications. This is a standard procedure for some jobs and entry on to certain academic courses. Previous work experience could be checked by requesting confirmation of dates worked from previous employers – if they are still in existence. Careful questioning, based on a structured approach, could be used to check the validity of reported job experiences, although this is clearly not bomb proof. The most difficult area to expose is always the information that has been omitted – do students have any creative ideas? There is clearly a balance between the effort required in checking CV information and the risk associated with appointing someone who is not as they appear on their CV. What criteria would students use to determine the jobs where significant checking should take place – is it level in the organisation or sensitivity of job (e.g. teacher, social worker, health worker)? There could be an argument that a well-constructed logical CV that appears to offer everything the organisation is requiring demonstrates that the candidate appreciates exactly what the organisation needs. This, it could be argued, shows high levels of understanding, good selling skills, flexibility, intelligence and resourcefulness.

2   *Application forms can sometimes elicit better information than CVs as they pose some direct questions that the CV may otherwise not address. However CVs remain highly popular. What advantages are there in using CVs for both the potential employee and the potential employer?*

For the employee there is the opportunity to choose a structure which enables them to demonstrate their strengths to best advantage. Also once written the same CV can be used with a tailored covering letter to apply for a range of jobs. This saves time compared with completing an application form. Some keen applicants will vary their CV to meet the demands of the job they are applying for, but even so this is usually less work than filling out an application form and does give them the chance to show themselves in the best light.

For the employer the CV demonstrates how well an individual can put their case together (i.e. how logical, persuasive, professionally presented it is). Also skills and experiences may appear on the CV which the employer may not have asked about on an application form or detailed in a person specification. These skills may or may not be immediately relevant to the job in question, but they may also have relevance to the potential of the individual in the organisation, and inform the employer on how flexibly this potential employee could be used.

Students may of course come up with other ideas. It may be worth while holding a discussion around how students approach their own CVs, and the methods they use to show themselves in the best light.

CHAPTER 13 STAFF RETENTION

This chapter is new to the fifth edition. Here we bring together material on different aspects of staff retention, a field which has gained in importance as labour markets have tightened up in recent years. The chapter starts by introducing the subject, looking at the impact of high turnover and the case for making its reduction a priority. We also look at recent turnover trends in the UK as whole, identifying for which groups job mobility has tended to increase and for which it has decreased. Later sections focus on the causes of staff turnover, at costing methods and at some of the more common approaches used to improve retention rates.

Additional teaching material

While the chapter focuses on the cost and causes of employee turnover, it does not reflect on how an organisation can/should go about investigating why people are leaving. We suggest that this issue can be effectively approached by inviting students to read and debate the following article. Here, the most common diagnostic tool used, the exit interview, is evaluated and subjected to some criticism.

Catharsis with your cards: Exit interviews with departing employees help companies to learn about themselves.

By Adrian Furnham, *Financial Times,* 28 August 2001

Some companies worry about high staff turnover; others clearly wish they had more. Organisations such as fast food outlets and insurance companies learn to live with fast staff turnover as a matter of course. But when an organisation begins to feel it is losing its best people, haemorrhaging its talent or simply experiencing a sudden loss from particular departments or sections, questions have to be asked.

Most managers have their own theories as to why staff leave. These may include poor pay, lack of career advancement or simply a poor selection decision in the first place. But others are not so sure and conduct some informal research. This usually involves little more than an interview with those who voluntarily quit rather than being fired or made redundant.

The theory is that such interviews can simultaneously fulfil a number of functions. They supposedly help an organisation to modify causes of attrition and other festering corporate problems. They can help some people because they give them a chance to let off their anger or disappointment in front of someone who is willing to listen.

In this sense the exit interview is more about damage control and prevention. At the most mundane level, exit interviews are about 'leaving protocol', including the orderly and sensible recovery of the employer's property (passes, badges, etc.) and ensuring that buildings and accounts remain secure.

So how do they work? The exit interviewer is usually chosen from the human resources department rather than from line managers. Ideally, they will be benevolent, avuncular 'good listeners' who take the side of the departing employee. They will be trained to act like clinicians and counsellors, being non-judgmental and focused entirely on the employee and his or her experience.

They have a set of standard, open-ended questions, which include: 'How did you feel you were managed during your time with us?'; 'In general, how do you feel this organisation is run?'; 'What could have persuaded you to stay with us another five years?'; 'What did you enjoy most/least about your time with us?'; 'How would you rate the work climate/corporate culture?' and, lastly, 'What are the main motives for your leaving?'

What is interesting about these questions is that they should all have been asked earlier – probably by the boss during an appraisal. The fact that no one asked the questions is no doubt a partial indicator of why the person has chosen to leave.

Interviewers should expect the unexpected emotional outburst: rage, tears, shouting. They should take rough notes, including whether they would hire the person if they reapplied for a job; or, more poignantly, what lessons could be learnt for hiring others in the future.

Part of the agenda of the exit interview is to understand the leaver's view of his or her compensation and benefits package and to influence it where this would be appropriate.

The factors influencing departure are well known: unhappiness at the place of work, combined with the attraction of another job. Factors cited include quality of supervision; relations with co-workers and subordinates; workload; job security; flexibility of hours; salary and benefits; location/commuting distance and personal or family matters.

From the employer's point of view, the idea of the exit interview is eminently sensible. In fact, it benefits the employer much more than the employee. It can gather useful information, soothe psychological wounds and prevent people turning into whistle-blowers and 'terrorists' who may subvert the organisation's reputation after they have left.

But from the point of view of the job-leaver, it has few benefits. It is tempting, when faced by a sympathetic senior person in the organisation, to unload the frustration and fury one has built up over the years.

The release of emotions may feel cathartic at the time but it is probably ill-advised in the long run. It is unwise to burn your bridges if you are in a small world, town or sector: remember, the organisation takes notes on what you say at the exit interview.

The best piece of advice is twofold: dissimulate or keep quiet. Do not say that your work was humdrum, stressful or tedious . . . talk of moving on to new challenges to upgrade your portfolio and extend your horizons.

Human resources practitioners are told that a good exit interview may help to limit costly legal action and other bad publicity instigated by a disgruntled employee. Remember: the notes of the exit interviewer could always be Exhibit A in some file somewhere.

One of the main problems of the interview is timing. People in the grieving business talk of a wet and a dry ceremony. The burial/cremation is full of shock and tears; the gathering to celebrate someone's life, held six months later, is more measured and more balanced. The emotional stress of leaving (even in the most happy circumstances) can lead to distorted, unreliable exchanges from both parties.

Resentment overcomes reason; emotion overcomes evaluation. The grieving process takes time and people can reflect more accurately on what they miss, have lost and feel. Thus it may be best to have an exit interview between six and nine months after the person has left. They may be invited out to or back to lunch to discuss the issues the company wants to know about. The advice for employees remains the same but from the company point of view it means they may gather some really useful intelligence from the delayed exit interview if they know what they are doing.

The author is professor of psychology at University College, London

Copyright © The Financial Times Limited 2001. Reproduced with permission.

Questions for discussion

1   What reasons for leaving are likely to be freely divulged in an exit interview by a person who has resigned? Which are most likely to be concealed?

2   Apart from the suggestion made in the article that exit interviews should be held some months after the resignation has taken effect, what else could be done to help ensure that they are a forum for the useful and accurate exchange of information?

3   Aside from exit interviews, what other methods can be used by employers in order to establish the main reasons for turnover among different employee groups?

Feedback

1   *What reasons for leaving are likely to be freely divulged in an exit interview by a person who has resigned? Which are most likely to be concealed?*

The reasons most likely to be freely divulged are those which do not reflect poorly on the conduct of either the employer or the employee. These would include the 'outside factors' described in Chapter 13, but could also be organisational issues outside the control of the department or business unit in which the person has worked (e.g. teachers, health workers and police disliking the administrative burden imposed by government).

Those most likely to be concealed are factors which reflect badly on the person or which make it look as if they are leaving for a trivial reason (e.g. not being up to certain aspects of the job, personality clash with a fellow worker), or which involve criticism of the organisation, its practices or individual managers. A major reason for leaving is a poor working relationship with the immediate line manager. Often this is not picked up in exit interviews at all because the person resigning is uncomfortable about stating it or because they want good future references.

2   *Apart from the suggestion made in the article that exit interviews should be held some months after the resignation has taken effect, what else could be done to help ensure that they are a forum for the useful and accurate exchange of information?*

Key points to think about here are:

(a)   *Who does the interview* – it is best if it is someone whom the person resigning does not know well but who is seen to have some authority in the organisation. The latter means that the interview is perceived to be significant and that some action may be taken about issues discussed. The former makes it more likely that honest (i.e. critical) remarks about the organisation and the real reasons for leaving will be made.

(b)   *The type of interview* – there is an argument for interviewers saying as little as possible during an exit interview and for keeping them as unstructured as possible. People usually leave for a complex mix of reasons (push and pull, personal and work based). The best way of picking up on all the factors and their significance in individual cases is to encourage the person resigning to talk through their decision-making process. When did they first consider leaving? How did the decision crystallise? Did any specific incidents contribute? When and why was the final decision taken? Did they look for an alternative job before deciding to leave or the other way round? That way the factors are revealed spontaneously rather than being suggested by questions put by the interviewer.

(c)   *When to do the interview* – the last day is not the best time. This is because it tends to be a day when emotions play a part in people's mood. Leaving parties are held, cards presented, generous speeches made in front of colleagues, etc. It is not a time for rational judgement and coolheaded expression. More than a week or two before the leaving date is too early because the working relationship is still psychologically in place, there will thus be a reluctance to make statements which reflect badly on organisational practices or individual managers. The beginning of the last week is a good time.

3   *Aside from exit interviews, what other methods can be used by employers in order to establish the main reasons for turnover among different employee groups?*

Attitude surveys, asking colleagues why people left, destination analyses, pay surveys, questionnaires sent to ex-employees, published surveys on turnover among professional groups.

CHAPTER 14 ENDING THE CONTRACT

The content of Chapter 14 is largely legal, because the law of unfair dismissal is now so central in determining all issues relating to dismissal in the UK. The law is surveyed generally, with the focus placed on the potentially fair reasons for dismissal and interpretations of the term 'reasonableness' in this context. Shorter sections towards the end of the chapter look at the written statement of reasons, constructive dismissal, notice periods and wrongful dismissal. There is also a section, which does not have a legal flavour, on the subject of retirement.

Additional teaching material

Here are three short case scenarios for students to read and consider. Each raises one or more important legal issues in the field of dismissal. They will find it helpful to refer to the relevant sections of Chapter 14 when thinking about each situation. Specific questions and/or activities are provided after each scenario has been described, together with tutor feedback.

Case 14.1

You work as a human resource manager in a large NHS hospital. One day you receive a call from a nurse manager asking for an urgent meeting to discuss a disciplinary matter. Earlier in the day a patient complained that some of his personal possessions had disappeared from a bedside cabinet. The items missing include a watch and a credit card. Both were subsequently discovered in a locker used by a nursing auxiliary called Michelle Wilson, who had been working on the ward the previous night. Ms Wilson has been employed at the Trust for three years and has an impeccable disciplinary record, but she has recently talked to colleagues about financial worries.

Given the above information, how would you proceed in dealing with this matter? What would you ensure was done in order to ensure that the Trust was able to defend itself effectively at any subsequent Employment Tribunal hearing?

Case 14.2

Assume that you have just started working as a Human Resources Manager in a firm of accountants. A total of 150 people are employed on a single site. On your first day one of the partners telephones you to say that he intends to dismiss a junior accountant later that day on grounds of gross misconduct. The employee's name is Mark Harris. The reason for the dismissal is the discovery that extensive use has been made of an office telephone line for private purposes. During the last quarter, calls to the value of £200 were made from Mark Harris's extension to a mobile phone owned by his girlfriend.

What are the major legal issues that need to be taken into consideration in a situation such as this? What questions would you need to ask the partner before advising him about the intended dismissal?

Case 14.3

Edwina Morris is employed as a catering supervisor by the Southington Borough Council School Meals Service. This is a senior role which involves managing two teams of staff based in different locations on a single school site.

Edwina has now been away from work for nine months because of a serious injury she sustained during a car accident last year. She wears a neck brace and suffers severe pain whenever she walks. In order to reduce the pain she takes prescribed medicines which cause her to have dizzy spells from time to time. She also has a tendency to become tired in the late afternoon because of the drugs. Her long-term medical prognosis is reasonable, but her doctor is unable to estimate if or when she will be fit enough to return to her job.

She was paid a full salary during the first six months of her illness, since when she has moved on to half pay. According to council policy, her pay will cease altogether after twelve months. She will then have to claim State Incapacity Benefit.

Edwina's manager comes to see you in your capacity as Human Resources Manager. He states that, unless there is a marked improvement in Edwina's condition between now and the first anniversary of her car accident, he intends to dismiss her on grounds of ill health.

What advice would you give the manager? What further information would you need in order to give accurate advice on the Council's position?

Feedback

Case 14.1

The main points students should make are as follows:

• This is a likely case of misconduct (i.e. a potentially fair reason for dismissal).

• Because theft is involved it is likely to be gross misconduct (i.e. could lead to summary dismissal).

• There is sufficient evidence reasonably to suspect Michelle Wilson.

• She has over a year's service, so could bring an unfair dismissal claim if the matter is poorly handled.

• The correct approach is to suspend Ms Wilson on full pay pending investigation.

• Carry out a full investigation, interviewing relevant witnesses, taking statements, etc.

• Arrange a disciplinary hearing within a few days, informing Ms Wilson of the time and place in writing, of the offence she is accused of having committed and of her right to be accompanied by a union official or work colleague.

• Put the charge to her at the hearing, allowing her the right to state her case.

- Decide whether or not to dismiss.

- Inform Ms Wilson of the decision, and her right to appeal.

- Take notes throughout to produce for an Employment Tribunal if necessary.

Case 14.2

The main points students should make are as follows:

- This can only definitely be considered gross misconduct if employees have been made fully aware that they have no right to make private use of the firm's telephones.

- Therefore there is a need to urge caution and check whether:

  (a)   there is a well-understood policy in place;

  (b)   Mark Harris has been warned previously.

- If not, this would need to be treated as ordinary misconduct.

- Need to have a hearing, give Mr Harris the right to be accompanied and to state his case.

- Issue a formal warning and confirm this in writing.

- A possibility would be to require Mr Harris to pay for the cost of the calls.

- If he had been warned previously OR was acting in breach of well-communicated firm rules, it can be treated as gross misconduct (using a procedure such as that in Case 14.1).

- Consistency may be a factor here (i.e. tribunals expect that all employees are treated equally in matters of discipline). Therefore before taking disciplinary action it is necessary to check that other employees are not regularly using the firm's phones to make private calls and are being allowed to do so.

Case 14.3

The main points students should make are as follows:

- This is a case in which dismissal on grounds of capability is being considered (i.e. a potentially fair reason for dismissal).

- According to the law of unfair dismissal it would be permissible to dismiss Ms Morris, provided she had been warned of the likelihood and given the opportunity to state why this should not occur.

- In this case, however, the timescales and nature of her injuries mean that she would probably be considered as disabled under the terms of the Disability Discrimination Act 1997.

- There is thus a need to make all attempts to make 'reasonable adjustments' to enable her to work.

- In consultation with her, the employer should thus explore whether there are circumstances in which she could work either in her original job or in another one.

- There is a need to consider redesigning the job, altering its location, shortening the hours, permitting some duties to be carried out at home, adjusting office accommodation, etc.

- Only once these possibilities have been given serious consideration and ruled out as impractical, is it safe to dismiss.

- Some form of early retirement could also be considered if Ms Morris is a member of the Council's occupational pension scheme.

CHAPTER 15 INTERACTIVE SKILL: SELECTION INTERVIEWING

This chapter takes a detailed and very practical look at selection interviewing in all its main aspects. Types of questions are explored as are forms of selection interview. We also look at the different purposes of interviews and at the process by which candidates and interviewees should prepare themselves ahead of time.

The focus is on the conduct of the selection interview *from the perspective of the interviewer*. This will probably arouse more interest than any other topic in the book, due to the varied stories that members of the group will want to tell, but they need to read this chapter as interviewers not as interviewees.

Additional teaching material

Exercise 15.1

Reverting to the comments about the two-way process of selection in Chapter 12, discuss with the whole group the three suggested purposes of the interview. Do they regard the list as correct, idealistic or incomplete?

Exercise 15.2

Below is a briefing for a practical exercise that students can carry out in the lecture room. Try running the practical exercise in pairs. If this is to work effectively, it is advisable to reassure students before they start that there will be no plenary session at the end: the exercise is self-contained and they either learn from it or they don't. This should help them to benefit from the learning implicit in the exercises, while avoiding their apprehension about looking foolish.

Student brief

Here is a practical exercise in selection interviewing for you to carry out. For this exercise you need a co-operative, interested relative, or a *very* close friend, who would welcome interview practice.

Follow the sequence outlined in the chapter to give your partner practice in being interviewed for a job, and giving yourself practice in interviewing and note-taking. You need first to agree at least the broad parameters of the post.

After the interview, discuss your mutual feelings about the process around questions such as:

Selector

- Did you ever feel you were being misled? When? Why?

- Did you feel the interview got out of your control? When? Why?

- How could you have avoided the problem?

- How was your note-taking?

- What, if anything, made you bored or cross?

- What did you find most difficult?

- How comprehensive are the data you have collected?

Candidate

- Were you put at your ease?

- Were you at any time inhibited by the selector?

- Did you ever mislead the selector? When? How?

- Did the selector ever fail to follow up important points? When? Which?

- Were you in any way disconcerted by the note-taking?

- Has the selector got a comprehensive set of data about you, so that you could feel any decision made about you would be soundly based?

- What did you think of the interview experience?

Now swap roles.

PART III CASE STUDY FEEDBACK

1   Information on all individuals currently employed. Information on the new organisational structure, jobs to be done and criteria for job holders.

Relevant employee information would include:

(a)   performance levels of all staff;

(b)   relevant qualifications, experience and specialist expertise of all staff;

(c)   assessment of potential of all staff;

(d)   length of service of all staff;

(e)   for staff in the south, the willingness of managerial and professional staff to move north (given an outline of the way that the move would be managed);

(f)   for staff in the north, the willingness of all staff to move/commute;

(g)   any preferences for redundancy/early retirement;

Some of this information may be difficult to collect, written inconsistently, or totally unavailable. Collecting it will, to some extent, be dependent on the working relationships between managers of the two companies.

2   Some of the issues that will need to be considered are:

(a) The need to take and understand the views/perspectives of the new senior management team. (It is likely that by the time you have your brief the alignment of senior management to new roles will be complete.)

(b) The need to design a process which provides the best opportunity for the most appropriate staff to be retained by the company.

(c) The need to use a process which will cause least damage to the loyalty and commitment of those who will be staying with the company – the survivors. The way that any redundancies are handled may well have an impact on this.

(d) The need to provide support and as much advance warning as possible for those who will be made redundant. The possible outsourcing of redundancy support.

(e) The need to make geographical relocations as painless as possible – forms of support that will be available.

(f) Estimated costs – what cost limitations are there?

(g) Whether to deal with the northern staff and southern staff differently – i.e. to retain all northern staff and slot into the new structure, and then select from the southern staff for the remaining posts – or to treat both groups the same.

(h) The speed with which decisions can be made. Although a clear limit has been given, within this the more quickly staff know what is happening to them, the better, as uncertainty will cause problems.

(i) Communication with all employees – how will employees be kept informed of what is happening to their employment? Where can they go to ask questions?

(j) Forms of interim support while there is still some uncertainty around, and perhaps for some time following.

(k) The need for induction training for new employees.

(l) Whether to outsource the new manual staff that will be needed.

3   There are many options for proceeding. One might be:

(a)   Immediately allocate middle management roles in conjunction with the senior management team.

(b)   Pay salary in lieu of notice plus generous redundancy/retirement settlement with outplacement services to the middle managers who are not required.

(c)   Confirm that the 300 specialist staff have jobs to go to in the north, as they are very difficult to substitute.

(d)   Communicate to other employees the timescales and process for selecting for other roles.

(e)   Ask for any requests for early retirement/voluntary redundancy.

(f)   Use open competition – i.e. everyone has to apply for roles in the new organisation (even if they are applying for their own jobs).

Problems with this approach may be:

•   resentment from the northern staff, as they didn't expect their jobs to be at risk;

•   those who elect redundancy or to retire may be the very staff the business needs to keep;

•   the specialist staff may not move north without some inducement.

CHAPTER 16 STRATEGIC ASPECTS OF PERFORMANCE

This chapter begins by exploring the way that our understanding of performance has changed and some of the influences on this change in thinking. We go on to consider current views of performance in the light of the three approaches to HR strategy which we identified in Chapter 3 – best practice; fit; and the resource-based view. In particular we concentrate on the recent American and UK research, and explore the usefulness of the 'bundles' approach. We progress to considering the mechanisms by which HR policies and practices may affect performance levels, and focus on the concept of commitment. Next we briefly review a range of performance initiatives and broadly place them as having an organisational, individual or team focus. These are followed up in Chapters 17,18 and 19. Finally we consider the barriers to change in terms of creating a performance-oriented organisation, and offer some broad recommendations for running a successful performance initiative.

Additional teaching material

Exercise 16.1

The following short article by Neil Britten warns about the dangers for organisations which fail to take a strategic approach to performance management. While the focus is on performance generally, well beyond the narrow HR field, the observations made have important implications for HR specialists. Discussion questions and feedback are provided at the end of the article.

INSIDE TRACK: A bigger picture of performance: Managers often neglect strategic goals when measuring how their company is doing

By Neil Britten, *Financial Times*, 7 August 2001

Imagine you must take a car journey from London to Paris. You estimate it should take six hours, you have a map and your car is well maintained and has a full tank of fuel. There are some restrictions on this journey, however. You may look only at the speedometer and the fuel gauge. There are no road signs and no broadcast warnings of traffic congestion. You set off and after two hours, having made good speed, you stop to assess your progress. Surprise. You are not at Dover and the map you started with does not show you where you are now. There is nowhere close by to refuel. As in our fictitious journey, performance measurement in most businesses is good at showing how things are going now but poor at showing how they will be in future. The reason is that two sorts of performance must be measured. One type, organisational performance, shows how the organisation is doing today and is analogous to speed, fuel consumption and the state of the car. Strategic performance measurement, however, is about how well the organisation will perform. It is like knowing you need a new map before discovering you are lost. The recent misfortunes of Marconi, the UK electronics company, illustrate how damaging it can be when a company is taken by surprise on its strategic journey.

Recently completed studies in the UK and the US highlight the shortcomings of performance measurement. Our own recent research, involving 27 UK-based companies such as BP, CGNU,

Kingfisher and Vodafone, shows that many struggle to choose the right measures and targets and the right performance measurement and management systems (PMMSs). The study also shows a lack of ability among some organisations to make use of what is measured. In the US study, 80 per cent of respondents believed PMMSs should help achieve results but did not and 65 per cent rated their PMMSs as poor or merely 'adequate' for helping strategy deployment. Our findings show a similar picture.

There is no shortage of PMMS techniques. Half of our interviewees claimed to use at least 10 different approaches. There is no 'silver bullet' but some better practices are emerging. The Balanced Scorecard* is an increasingly popular approach that goes beyond pure financial measurement to include such elements as customers, human resources and innovation. About half of our sample claimed to use it. Some forecasters believe more than 70 per cent of US-based companies will be using it within two years.

Given this popularity, companies must see advantages to the Balanced Scorecard. Yet they typically have only one or two years' experience of the technique. It must be correctly applied, which is not always easy. Key performance indicators (KPIs) are also widely used. These are measures chosen to reflect performance in high-impact areas, especially in operations such as error rates. Balanced Scorecard gurus tend to be dismissive of KPIs, pointing out that using too many measures without any organising principle leads to 'measurement paralysis' – although this criticism can equally be applied to the way many use the Balanced Scorecard.

Although KPIs are effective when used within a clear structure, there are dangers. The KPIs for operational monitoring are often unrelated to strategic objectives. They can be too financially focused or defined without clear accountability. Whatever the theory about balanced scorecards and KPIs, research shows that the practice often falls short of expectations. Also, most approaches fail to measure strategic performance.

Executives need better advance warning of the need to reappraise their strategy – as demonstrated in a recent survey, when Canadian chief executives headed their wish list with a call for better strategic indicators. Another gap is the measurement of 'strategy deployment', i.e. how effectively you are progressing towards your strategic objectives. Organisational performance is no substitute because it measures this only after the fact. For example, sales growth is a good organisational measure of the success of a strategy to launch a new product or service. But it is not forward-looking. It could not predict failure to meet the target launch date, say.

The remedies are not complex but they require sustained management effort. Aim to connect the way strategy is formulated with the way goals are set and communicated, with the choice and use of PMMS tools, with performance review and reward mechanisms. Emphasise getting things done. As Lou Gerstner observed on becoming chief executive of International Business Machines: 'This organisation had plenty of great strategies – it didn't successfully implement any of them.'

A good strategy is insufficient – you need to manage its deployment and for that you need effective strategic performance measurement. Success comes not only from having a great map but also from completing the journey.

The Balanced Scorecard (1996), by Robert Kaplan and David Norton, Harvard Business School Press.

The writer is managing director of BLN Associates.

nbritten@blnassociates.co.uk.

Copyright © Neil Britten 2001. Reproduced with permission.

Questions for discussion

1   What problems with performance measurement does this article identify?

2   Consider you own organisation. Which of these problems are apparent in the organisation's approach to performance measurement? How might the problems be overcome?

Feedback

1   *What problems with performance measurement does this article identify?*

Guideline answer

- Difficulty in choosing the right measures and targets.
- Difficulty in choosing the right performance measurement and management systems.
- Not making use of what is measured.
- Although companies may use the balanced scorecard, they have little experience and it is important that the technique is applied correctly.
- Some organisations use too many measures, especially if they use key performance indicators.
- Measures need to be related in a framework, and organisations do not always do this.
- The last two problems may result in 'measurement paralysis'.
- There is usually a gap in measuring strategy deployment – how effectively the organisation is progressing to meet its strategic goals.

2   *Consider you own organisation. Which of these problems are apparent in the organisation's approach to performance measurement? How might the problems be overcome?*

Guideline answer

No specific guidelines here, but it may be worth while also to get students to consider the impact of the organisation's current performance measurement practices on organisational performance. If anyone is from the health service, or even if not, the 'hospital waiting list' example may be a good one to discuss.

Exercise 16.2

Introduce the range of factors which affect performance (such as culture, leadership, empowerment, commitment, etc.) and then use buzz groups to identify how students' organisations have approached these factors (or not), including what banner is used (e.g. TQM, JIT) .

Divide into groups to discuss the following case study which they should have read in advance of the session. The case study includes extracts of interviews with three different organisations. On the basis of these interview extracts ask the groups to identify the issues and problems of introducing organisation-wide initiatives; and to discuss the HR role in these.

EXTRACTS FROM THREE INTERVIEWS IN DIFFERENT ORGANISATIONS

EXTRACT 1 (Organisation 1)

(Investors in People – is that something you're going for here?)

We're trying to, yes. We haven't got very far. I spoke to the TEC yesterday with another excuse, erm … we'd like to do it. I'd like to improve the way we deliver training here, particularly. The problem we've got is it's not a good time to do it when you're making so many people redundant, so I'm just holding on at the moment, because it just doesn't seem fair to banner wave at the same time as making 60 or 70 people redundant.

(Was it a Personnel decision?)

No, it was proposed at the TQM steering group as a good way of improving our culture here and improving training delivery and it was accepted as a proposal.

(So would it be Personnel that would be driving it?)

Yes.

(Do the words learning organisation mean anything here?)

The blunt answer is no. It ought to is the answer, it doesn't … er … we do have some processes which allow learning to take place like project management, post-project reviews, where it went well, where it went wrong, the typical learning processes, but that was not done as part of some grand scheme of making us a learning organisation. It was just good management practice. But we do have as part of our TQM programme a number of strands of benchmarking but there's nothing specific. It's not something I want to take on board as, well, you've got to be really careful about something that, er, perhaps academics don't realise, or maybe they do, but you've got to be really careful about having a fad. Now we've had TQM here for about four or five years now, and it needs to be TQM for 15 years really. I don't mind pulling out other things, there's no problem with looking at what's coming in the literature about learning organisations and integrating that into your TQM programme. What we can't do is say, ah well we've stopped doing TQM, now we're a learning organisation or a re-engineered organisation or whatever. So, yes, it will mean something to us because some of the ideas are sound, but I mean, it's basically standard ISO9000 quality procedure to review your projects and look for ways of improving them, and I now see that creeping into the learning organisation literature. I'm not trying to be cynical, but you just have to be careful that you have a focus and you keep on that focus for a long time.

(Is that so the culture isn't damaged or is that so Personnel keeps its credibility as a function?)

Oh it's to make sure that the cultural change works, if you keep changing where you're going, you're never going to get there. The whole key to change success is commitment from management, if people think that management are committed to this change it will eventually happen, I think. A good way to show that you're not committed is to keep changing what you're committed to every five years, because that doesn't send a signal of commitment, it sends a signal that someone at the top is reading the *Harvard Business Review* and thinks, 'Ah well, we'd better be doing that.'

(So is TQM something that really integrates the business, that the business as a whole is going for?)

Yes, it is integrated, it does form ... er ... part of the planning process for the year is based around policy deployment which is another TQM buzzword which is all about a process of setting goals for the organisation and the business units within it, and we do quite a lot of training, and it does form quite a significant part of 'the way we do things around here'.

(Does Personnel have quite a central role in that?)

It does because I was the change manager really. Over the last three or four years I've been the change manager. I've worked in a number of departments over those years, both on line and off the line, and during those years I've kept the change management responsibility. I happen to be in HR. I happen to be responsible for the change management process for TQM, I chair the committee, so HR gets more involved because I'm in HR now. I suppose that as a change manager you tend to involve the area which you're most involved with yourself. I'm now in HR.

EXTRACT 2 (Organisation 2)

The TQM thing is another question entirely in terms of to what extent has this company or any other really embraced total quality, and it's in fact something we're wrestling with there at the moment, because Organisation 2 still hasn't achieved that transformation which a real TQM mindset can help you get there. But if for example Organisation 2 were to break through on that, yes it has identified that leadership and management style are key drivers in TQM – HR is very much involved in that in terms of trying to engender and develop those behaviours through a whole raft of HR techniques. So yes, we would be very much involved in that.

(You don't have any quality committee do you?)

No, everybody in the process has to wear that hat.

(And how do you think that's going? Do you think you've achieved a 'quality-orientated culture'?)

No. I can be the company's greatest critic, even though I've worked here for the best part of 23 years, but our approach towards total quality is still a little bit initiative led. We've got IIP, we've got most of the support functions including the whole technology division here having

IS0900, and in terms of if you were to were to walk into, for example, our printing and stationery department, which is a complete facility employing around 100 staff, a very upmarket facility there, they are employing 'just in time' control techniques. It's all there – but would you say that is indicative and running right through the very core of Organisation 2? The answer is no quite frankly … Our approach towards IIP was, what are we doing this for and what are the opportunities here to make something better as a result of it, and we identified very early on that we had a serious problem at the bottom end of Organisation 2 in terms of our front line delivery – in terms of the place that training and development has on the agenda in our branch offices. We also were not happy either with communications, top to bottom, so we were wrestling with those three things in three separate parts of the company, when all of a sudden IIP came along, and we thought, ah, and I'm glad that we can hang it all on that. So we actually had significant added value out of IIP. I've come to the conclusion that it's down to how bad is the need. I mean, how badly do you need some of these things to be fixed? In our case we were desperate to try and fix some of these things, and IIP came along at just the right time. But I think that there are those companies who are just going to get the badge, but I guess they are going to find that they are disappointed with the added value.

EXTRACT 3 (Organisation 3)

(If there is a business-led objective, like moving to TQM or business re-engineering, where would Personnel come into that?)

Well, we've got a couple on the go at the moment – we've got TQM operating here and we're about to go to IIP. We're part of the way through that and we've been leading the process of planning it and making sure that the actions are actually carried out. So we act as facilitators, planners and change agents. But the actual actions are undertaken by the line managers.

(Did you have a say at board level as to where that was going?)

Personnel did, yes, in a sense that it was initiated by the Personnel Director (UK) and sold to the Managing Director who then took it on board. It went that way round.

(How far are you down the line with IIP?)

We're half way through an action plan to close the gap. We're probably about half way to achieving the standard 'IT'! I think the assessment is lighter this year, we hope. It's no good going in for the assessment unless you're damn certain you're going to get it, otherwise we wouldn't do it. So we're probably looking at the back end of this calendar year … Yes, there is a feeling that IIP is becoming more of a – dare I say it – a green stamp of approval rather than what it was intended to be, or the way we're utilising it, which is to change the culture of the place. We're actually doing things and forcing managers to operate in a different way – communicate, involve and so on and so forth – to sort of empower rather than direct, which is where they were at, and we're using the IIP process to actually effect that change.

(How well is that going?)

Well again, it's like all of these things. You have more success with some managers than others. Some will grasp the concept and go along readily with it. Others really struggle because all their skills lie in another direction and some of them adopt new skills more readily than others – but we're getting there.

(Do the words 'learning organisation' mean anything here?)

I think if I were to try to introduce the concept of the learning organisation from where we're at at the moment I'd get blank looks. The organisation is still too much in the directional mode rather than the empowerment mode to actually understand what a learning organisation is, why you would need one or 'what would it do for us'! To be honest, they are heading towards it because of the concept of continuous improvement, but it would just be another piece of jargon. When I read my personnel management magazines I'm horrified at some of the hype around some of the things like a 'learning organisation'. The culture has to be right for it – there isn't a panacea that will fit every situation, every organisation – even every bit within a single organisation. Sometimes we run before the organisation is ready to run. If the organisation is only ready to walk then you should walk with it rather than try and drag it by the scruff of its neck into a running pace which it is not ready for. And I think we sometimes as a profession lose sight of the fact that all of this should be business need driven rather than just our profession saying 'isn't this a good idea?' I think you actually get far more credibility if you've identified or helped to identify a business need and then solve it. I think that's how we should get our credibility. The need for change should be a business need not someone wishing to adopt whatever the latest concept is.

CHAPTER 17 ORGANISATIONAL PERFORMANCE

This chapter focuses on two major contributions to performance improvement at the organisational level – total quality management and learning organisations. A third perspective, organisational development, is dealt with more briefly at the end of the chapter. In considering total quality management, we review how the concept and focus has changed since the early influences of Japan and quality circles. We also note the varied ways in which it continues to be interpreted and applied. Moving on from this we identify key elements of management practice which need to be present to give total quality management the best chance of success. Also incorporated is a more critical review of what actually happens in practice, and some of the difficulties in sustaining this approach.

The development and importance of the learning organisation concept is described, and the difference between organisational learning and learning organisations is explored. We review a range of well-known models such as those from Pedler, Burgoyne and Boydell and Senge, and a critique of the concept is also included.

Additional teaching material

For this exercise you will need to download the following article from the internet. It can be accessed through the *Financial Times* website: www.ft.com.

Making knowledge visible: KM projects are known to add value to an organisation. The question, is, however, how much?

By Prusak Larry, *The Financial Post,* Published in (Canada) 24 July 2001.

Discussion questions

1   What possible methods are there to collect and disseminate knowledge in the organisation?

- What does your organisation do and how effective is this?

- How does you organisation encourage people to use expertise located elsewhere in the organisation?

2   Are informal discussions, social occasions and emails actively encouraged or discouraged in your organisation?

- In what ways are they encouraged or discouraged?

- Should these activities be actively encouraged? Why?

- In what ways could such behaviours be encouraged?

Feedback

1   Students are likely to suggest databases (of various types), inventories, networks, email links, knowledge-sharing meetings. The question is, how do you encourage employees to take part in each of these activities/facilities?

    In terms of their own organisation ensure that students not only describe what is available, but say how it is used, and why, and how effective this appears to be. The third part of the question need not be limited to activities specifically labelled knowledge management – but can be addressed in a general sense, as it's the activity not the label that is most important.

2   The purpose of this set of questions is to encourage thought and debate about the contribution that informal communication makes to knowledge sharing and why this is so. This is not an area that is easy to actively manage, and yet there is an argument that such informal communication is critical if knowledge is to be shared immediately and on an ongoing basis. While such communication may only apply to some aspects of knowledge sharing, ongoing informal communication is cheap, easy and relatively attractive (from the perspective of both the employee and employer), and therefore warrants attention.

CHAPTER 18   MANAGING INDIVIDUAL PERFORMANCE

This chapter begins by describing the basics of the performance cycle and the following part of the chapter concentrates on one aspect of this – performance review. We consider the different types of performance appraisal systems, in terms of how performance is measured. We include measurement of job objectives, competencies, tasks included in the job description, and also explain some more technical approaches such as BARS and BOS. We consider the range of purposes of appraisal systems and also critique the effectiveness of appraisal systems. The following section is devoted to the use of 360˚ feedback. The final part of the chapter explores performance management systems – a typical system is described and we review the advantages of such a system. We also consider the problems that may be encountered in implementation and critique the concept of performance management. Further details of the appraisal process and guidelines for carrying out an appraisal are found in Chapter 23.

Additional teaching material

The exercise for this chapter takes the form of a short case study. Discussion questions and feedback are provided at the end.

Introducing a new performance management system

A large organisation, which traditionally had a paternalistic approach and low levels of unionisation, decided to introduce a performance management system incorporating performance-related pay. This changed the nature of the previous incremental salary scales and led to the abolition of the annual cost of living related increase.

The new system incorporated an annual objective-setting process, ongoing review and annual assessment with a reward link. The annual assessment determined two things. First, whether the individual could move up the salary scale one increment, could move up two increments, would remain put or would move down one increment. There were careful descriptions related to performance which indicated which action should be taken in respect of each individual. This replaced the previous system where increments were automatic and there was no possibility of moving down an increment. Second, the assessment was translated into a grade (A–E) and each grade was linked to an amount of performance-related pay, expressed as a percentage of current salary. There were however limits on the number of people in any department who could be put into each category. So, for example, A grade, which represented outstanding performance, was only available to 5 per cent of the staff in any department.

The system was introduced very quickly by the use of a consulting firm. However two years after implementation there are high levels of dissatisfaction from employees, and some line managers have also expressed serious concerns about their role in the system and the system itself.

To tackle the problem a different consulting firm was used as the previous one had disbanded. They carried out some research and established the following:

- Objectives were not always agreed at the beginning of the period, sometimes they were agreed at the end or not at all.

- Reviews were not generally carried out during the year.

- Those departments that did set objectives found high levels of competitiveness between staff and an unwillingness to support others.

- Changes to the incremental system were widely resented, except by a few high-flyers.

- There was less resentment with the PRP concept although many felt the system was not used fairly or consistently.

- Many employees, including line managers, did not understand why the system was introduced, others thought it was to do with cost cutting.

- All felt the grade limits were unfair.

- Employees did not feel line managers were objective in their assessments.

- Some line managers expressed discomfort with the process.

- Most employees felt their development needs were ignored.

- The reward levels were too small to motivate employees.

Questions for discussion

1   Given that the company wish to retain a performance management system, what issues would you recommend are addressed in reforming the system?

2   Explain and justify how you would change the system and how you would re-launch it.

Feedback

1   *Given that the company wish to retain a performance management system, what issues would you recommend are addressed in reforming the system?*

You should expect students to identify:

- the need for much more communication and explanation;

- the need to address concerns and allow staff to express these in an appropriate forum;

- the need for training, particularly for line managers, but also for employees;

- methods for ensuring fairness and consistency;

- methods for encouraging collaboration through the system rather than competition;

- methods of incorporating development into the system;

- exploration of whether the grading system and the link to reward are appropriate, and what alternatives there might be.

2 *Explain and justify how you would change the system and how you would re-launch it*

There are many possibilities here. The key is whether the new system and its launch address the issues defined above and that each part of the system and process is justified.

CHAPTER 19 TEAM PERFORMANCE

This chapter briefly reviews the growth of teamwork, and also raises concerns about its increasing use. Different types of organisational teams are then explored, and the characteristics of timespan, extent of interchangeability of staff, and the task and functional range of the team's remit are discussed. We describe in more detail the nature of production/service teams; cross-functional management teams; functional teams; and problem-solving teams. The following section is devoted to team effectiveness and we consider the selection of team members, Belbin's team roles, team leader and manager training, and team member training. We identify and discuss different approaches to team development.

Additional teaching material

The following articles report two cases which demonstrate the operational effectiveness of boards of directors. The first is a view from a Chief Executive of the shortcomings of the way that his board operates. The second relates the experiences of a new member of a board of directors. The cases are located in different companies. Exercises and discussion questions, together with feedback, are provided at the end.

Article 19.1

INSIDE TRACK: Boardroom rejects command and control: A successful manager must master persuasion and advocacy in order to become an effective director

By Stephen Schneider, *Financial Times*, 26 June 2001

One of the many stumbling blocks facing successful managers on entering the boardroom is how they handle the transition itself. The very characteristics that made an individual successful in an operational role may derail them when they reach the board.

A manager who has succeeded at the operational level will have employed command and control skills. Successful managers use positional power to get things done. For a board director, this is no longer appropriate: what is required is the effective use of personal power – the ability to influence others by reasoned argument and persuasion.

One client, a newly appointed marketing director aged 36, could not understand why his early contribution had not been well received by his board colleagues. A successful manager within the company for some time, he was unused to such a lacklustre response from colleagues. He had taken time to prepare for his first meeting, as making a strong first impression was important to him.

He soon realised that by taking his command and control tactics into the boardroom he had ensured that his approach would jar. His insistence on closing down the options, removing uncertainty and ambiguity, reaching a conclusion quickly and moving forward ran counter to what was expected of him in his new role.

The chairman repeatedly interrupted his meticulously planned presentation with: 'No, no, no. Don't rush to a conclusion. All we want you to do is to put forward your position on the issue. Let others probe and challenge your thinking.' What was important to the board was that by a process of challenge and debate it would eventually attain a collective view of the best way forward. The manager felt patronised, confused and perplexed at getting his footwork so wrong.

Boardroom effectiveness flows from a member's powers of persuasion by the exercise of advocacy skills. Status counts for nothing in the boardroom but argument and reason will have powerful results. Directors now carry onerous responsibilities – and indeed liabilities – so the commitment to a course of action by the board comes only from consensus about its suitability and acceptance of any likely consequences.

Such conviction will be gained only after a campaign of reasoned argument by the individual putting forward an idea or approach. That will be successful only if the individual can present the best case, balancing the upsides and downsides, the opportunities and the risks, and convince the board that the suggested way forward is the most appropriate.

Strategy is the process of positioning an organisation for future advantage. It requires deep understanding of internal and external factors. Leadership is the weapon that provides strategic impact. It demands the articulation of an argument so compelling that other people see its merits and are prepared to act on it. A retreat into the comfort zone of management, by exerting influence in a narrow area by a vested authority, is an abdication of leadership.

As for making the transition to becoming an effective leader for those entering the boardroom for the first time, the director must learn new types of behaviour, which cannot necessarily be learnt at business school. Indeed, some would argue that leadership cannot be taught at all. Although few boards offer any training, most are quick to point out the immediate rewards of having new directors who can make effective early contributions.

Another critical issue for fresh boardroom players concerns the confusion about what they can and cannot comment upon in the boardroom. There is a natural tendency among new board members – and indeed even among more experienced directors – to see their role as 'functional heroes' rather than 'trustees of the business'. Thus the board is treated as an operational team, addressing operational issues rather than 'matters of state'. This is a common mistake and may reduce boardroom effectiveness.

Members of the board should try to become familiar with all aspects of the business and should aspire to be as capable of advocating issues outside their own functional portfolio as within it. New appointees must learn to resist pursuing individual or narrow functional interests and must start to think in terms of collective responsibilities and detached objectivity.

The role of board director is to exercise judgment in areas outside his or her area of direct responsibility. The person who is on 'home turf' regarding a particular issue is there to give the facts, paint in the background and present the decision to be made – but it is for the board collectively to decide. As such, strategic perspectives are more relevant in the boardroom than the command of operational detail.

At the end of the day, the individual has to master the art of persuading the board. Ultimately – and this is in stark contrast to the relationship between manager and subordinate – it is the board that decides. The new game for the incoming director to master is all about advocacy skills and personal powers of persuasion, much as a barrister needs when seeking to convince a court. It is all about providing evidence, reaching conclusions and making recommendations – and not necessarily in that order. And, of course, a little personal charisma will certainly help.

The writer is managing director of CPS, an executive mentoring and boardroom development company

Article 19.2

Putting the team into top management

By Donald Hambrick, FT CareerPoint, 6 October 2000

Donald C. Hambrick is Samuel Bronfman Professor of Democratic Business Enterprise at Columbia University Graduate School of Business.

Two years had passed since my last visit to Richard, the chief executive of a large financial services firm. After our hellos, it quickly became clear that things had gone sour for him and the company in that time: 'We were riding high, doing so well. Then we hit a wall. Competitors started offering attractive bundled products to major customers; they started serving global accounts in an integrated way; and they beat us in developing electronic offerings. I'm embarrassed at how long it took us to figure out what was happening, and I'm angry at myself and my team for being unable to develop and deliver our responses.' Worse still, attempts to tackle things had failed: 'Whenever I try to get my top executives together to wrestle with these challenges, invariably one or more of the division presidents will argue that they're each aggressively dealing with them in their own units. But these problems call for company-wide action, not piecemeal initiatives. Frankly, I think we're paying a big price for the autonomy we've granted senior executives. They're each running their own fiefdoms. We can't get our act together.'

Regrettably, Richard's situation is not unique. He has no real top management team. Even though he calls his executive group a 'team', it has few team properties. And he is paying for it. When marketplace opportunities or threats call for co-ordination and unity of action, a company with a fragmented senior group will usually suffer dearly, as had Richard's.

The expression 'top management team' is a misnomer for the groups that exist at the apex of many firms. Many such groups are simply constellations of executive talent: individuals who rarely come together (and then usually for perfunctory information exchange), who rarely collaborate, and who focus almost entirely on their own part of the enterprise. Senior executives often sing the praises of teamwork at lower levels, but when it comes to themselves, they often exhibit aloofness and blinkered perspectives.

The problem of fragmentation at the top can be traced to a variety of factors. In some companies, chief executives are resistant to teamwork at the top level, fearing either that it amounts to an abdication of their leadership role or that it runs counter to their company culture of unit accountability and initiative. What these executives do not understand is that an effective top management team greatly extends the capabilities of the chief executive; it rarely dilutes them. A

90

well-functioning top team is an important complement to, not the antithesis of, business unit drive.

The meaning of teamwork

In an era requiring corporate coherence, companies have to orchestrate their activities at the highest levels, not just operations. They must promptly identify and diagnose the need for periodic company-wide changes and be able to execute those changes. Companies can do this only if their top executive groups have team properties, particularly what I call 'behavioural integration'.

Behavioural integration is urgently needed in the upper echelons. It describes the degree to which the senior management group engages in a mutual and collective way. It has three elements: the quantity and quality (richness, accuracy, timeliness) of information exchange among executives; collaborative behaviour; and joint decision-making. That is, a behaviourally integrated top management group – a real team – shares information, resources and decisions.

Having a top management group with these properties does not mean management by parliamentary body. It does not rule out having a strong chief executive, although it does rule out having one who serves as the broker or mediator in all senior executive interchanges or who attempts to formulate major changes alone. Also, behavioural integration doesn't rule out entrepreneurship by business units, although it does reject disjointed initiatives or those that are at cross-purposes to the bigger picture. In fact, because many executives seem so sceptical about teamwork at the top, it is useful to specify what behavioural integration is not.

It is not like-mindedness. Top executives should have differing experiences and perspectives. Behavioural integration capitalises on differences by providing forums of exchange and debate, not 'groupthink'. Nor is such behaviour the same as interpersonal appeal or friendship. Although outright antipathy among executives is harmful, chumminess is rare and is not necessary for integration. Finally, behavioural integration does not demand endless meetings. Some face-to-face contact is necessary, but extreme amounts are not.

Exercises and discussion questions

Based on these two reported experiences:

1   Design a development programme which helps to prepare senior managers to act as board directors.

2   Outline the main difficulties involved in developing such senior managers.

3   Consider what a Chief Executive could use to ensure that the board or senior team operate as a team.

Feedback

1   *Design a development programme which helps to prepare senior managers to act as board directors.*

In terms of content the following areas are likely to emerge:

- Developing persuasion and argument skills.

- Learning to hold back – learning to ask questions and debate issues and options – rather than coming to a premature conclusion.

- Information sharing.

- Understanding business functions other than one's own.

- Developing strategic thinking skills and a holistic view.

- Developing an understanding of the nature of collective responsibility.

- Understanding the role of the board.

Other factors to look for are timescale – is it reasonable for busy senior staff? balance between formal and informal methods; recognition of the nature of senior staff.

2   *Outline the main difficulties involved in developing such senior managers.*

The following types of issues might be expected to emerge:

- Time constraints.

- Difficulty in recognising that development is needed – (got this far without it, or got this far and don't need any more).

- More difficulty in being able to admit weaknesses.

- Likely to be highly task focused (if been successful in the organisation so far – could argue that it's these people who are more likely to be promoted) so might be resistance to a 'touchy-feely' approach to development.

- Need high level of facilitator skills and facilitator needs to be credible in terms of personal style and experiences.

(To take this topic further see question 3 and the article below)

3   *Consider what measures a Chief Executive could use to ensure that the board or senior team operate as a team.*

See further Hambrick article below.

Putting the team into top management (Part 2)

By Donald Hambrick, FT CareerPoint, 6 October 2000

What can be done?

If you believe your senior executive group needs to become more of a team, what should you do? Research suggests some promising initiatives. First, be sure the group has a clear identity. The group should have a name, even something as straightforward as executive committee or policy group. Membership needs to be clearly conveyed, not to establish an elite, but to allow members to identify with the team and to understand they are a part of it.

Second, assign real work to the group. If the group only convenes to share information or to review other people's work, there can be no sense of team commitment or energy. The senior group needs to roll up its sleeves and take on substantive tasks. Appropriate tasks include those that deal with company-wide marketplace challenges. Another job for the group to take on is retooling the company's performance management system (its evaluation, measurement, and incentive processes). One of the chief executive's key tasks is to look for suitable company-wide issues the group can tackle.

Third, be sure the group meets often enough to feel like a team. This is not as often as some people might expect. Once a month for half a day is usually sufficient. (If team members are located around the world, quarterly meetings plus video conferencing can suffice.) The group should have at least a couple of two-day meetings away from the office each year, at which difficult issues can be tackled in depth. In the process, familiarity and trust will be reinforced.

Fourth, pull executives out of their parochial zones. For instance, consider giving unit heads additional responsibilities for company-wide endeavours. These 'overlay' assignments can be temporary (such as heading up an e-commerce task force) or more continuous (overseeing a staff or support unit).

Another initiative, increasingly being used, is to rotate executives selectively, requiring them to take their experience and perspective to a new setting within the company. The objective, again, is to develop a senior team of executives with a company-wide perspective. For instance, Jorma Ollila, chief executive of Nokia, rotated several of his top executives about a year ago as a way of keeping them fresh and focused on company-wide opportunities.

Fifth, be sure executives have an incentive to be concerned about the whole. At least a third of incentive compensation should be tied to overall company performance. And a third of every executive's annual incentive reward should be paid in company stock or options. These are precisely the initiatives Louis Gerstner took at IBM to overcome the parochial behaviour of executives who had almost all of their pay riding on how well their units – and only their units – performed. Nothing is worse than asking executives to devote their efforts to the team but then rewarding them only for their own unit's performance.

93

Finally, the chief executive must set the tone. He or she must convey and reinforce norms of openness and constructive candour in the team. The chief executive must ensure disagreement and minority views are not penalised, and, above all, that healthy, sometimes heated, debate never becomes personal.

Implementing change

An integrated senior team is crucial not only to diagnosing the company's situation and formulating large-scale change, but also to implementing change. In fact, senior managers' attitudes and conduct always make the difference between successful and unsuccessful corporate transformation. Top executives particularly have an essential, and often overlooked, role as leading advocates of change.

In any large-scale organisational change, employees have four essential questions in their minds. Why do we have to change? Why is this the right change? Why do you think this organisation can handle the change? What are you going to do to help me through the change?

Answering these questions is a central challenge for leadership. However, the selling effort cannot succeed as a one-person endeavour. This is a job not just for the chief executive but for the whole top team. Tragically, the greatest obstacles in the internal effort to sell change are often the chief executive's own direct lieutenants – precisely the people who are supposed to lead the change. If even just one of these executives gives mixed signals to his or her department, the change effort may be doomed. Corporate transitions can succeed only if all the top executives commit themselves to convincing others of the wisdom and feasibility of the company's new direction.

Jack Welch's early days as head of General Electric provide an illustration. Once he had assembled a group of senior executives who agreed with important new themes (such as 'We will only be number one or two, or else we will sell it, fix it, or close it' and 'We believe in openness and candour'), the entire senior management group was sent to visit operations around the world and spread the message. Each of these executives spent several months doing this. It was critically important, of course, that the themes were reinforced by substantive actions, such as resource allocation, rewards, and staffing. But the role of the entire senior management team in mounting a unified campaign in support of the new direction was key to the transition GE experienced.

Summary

Like all resources, an effective senior team requires investment and time to develop. A team cannot be produced on command, particularly in a crisis. Therefore, the business head who wants more teamwork at the top must start today. Then, when a major market shift occurs, the top team will be able to comprehend and interpret the shift, formulate a strategic response and implement it.

Further reading

Hambrick, D.C. (1995) 'Fragmentation and the Other Problems CEOs Have With Their Top Management Teams', *California Management Review*, 37 (34).

Hambrick, D.C., Nadler, D.A., and Tushman, M.L. (eds) (1998) *Navigating Change: How CEOs, Top Teams, and Boards Steer Transformation*, Cambridge, MA: Harvard Business School Press.

Janis, I.L., and Mann, L. (1977) *Decision Making*, New York: Free Press.

Katzenbach, J.R. (1998) *Teams at the Top*, Cambridge, MA: Harvard Business School Press.

Nadler, D.A., Spencer, J.L., and Associates (1998), *Executive Teams*, San Francisco: Jossey-Bass.

CHAPTER 20 LEADERSHIP AND MOTIVATION

In this chapter we consider three fundamental approaches to understanding the nature of leadership. The first, and historically the earliest, is the trait approach which seeks to identify the characteristics of those who become leaders, although of late there has been a change of emphasis and the focus is now on identifying the traits an *effective* leader. The second approach focuses on the behaviour or style of the leader, and the emphasis here is on the 'best' style with an underlying assumption that the appropriate skills and behaviours can be learned. The third fundamental approach is based on the concept that different styles and behaviours will be appropriate in different circumstances and with different followers.

Following on from the basic approaches we consider the attention which has been given to transformational leadership and the more recent focus on post-heroic/empowering leadership. We conclude with a section which links the various leadership theories discussed to theories of motivation.

Additional teaching material

The following article by the editor of the *Financial Times* CareerPoint website focuses on leadership in the contemporary business environment and contrasts this with traditional conceptions of what makes a 'good leader'. The article also introduces readers to the website and its aims. At the end we provide discussion questions, an activity brief and lecturer feedback.

Leadership. Do you have what it takes?

By Richard Donkin, FTCareerPoint website, 15 January 2001

Work used to be something we were told to do by a supervisor. These days we're asked: or we're left to ourselves with our tasks outlined and restructured every now and again. The work is something that's expected of us.

Supervisors have been renamed team leaders and remodelled as mentors, coaches, guides, or simply points of reference. We're all managers now. Management has been developed down the line so that almost all of us manage something or someone, if only ourselves.

This devolution of management, its extension to every corner of the organisation, and its interpretation as something of an administrative function, has led management theorists to look for another quality that can differentiate management and the managed. This quality is leadership.

Top dogs

Leadership, like management, used to be something identified with top people. There were leaders and there were followers. Anybody could spot a leader by his title – general, king, president, prime minister, chief executive, headmaster. Anybody could name a leader – Nelson, Napoleon, Hannibal – we still tend to reach for military examples. Just look at the recent popularity of Sun Tzu the Chinese general whose strategies were devised around 500 BC.

But theorists such as Warren Bennis, the US leadership guru, have redefined leadership for the modern organisation. Whilst serving as the youngest lieutenant in the US army in World War Two, Bennis noticed that leadership did not necessarily go with rank. There were times he led from the front and there were times he, with the rest of his unit, relied on the experience and qualities of a platoon sergeant or a corporal.

As Dava Sobel observed in her book, *Longitude*, that would never have been acceptable to the Royal Navy in 1707 under Rear Admiral Sir Cloudesley Shovel, who had one of his seamen hanged for questioning the course he had set on a journey back to England. The seaman's concern was valid. Sir Cloudesley's ship was wrecked on the Scilly Isles with the loss of all hands.

The vision thing

Bennis sought something more in leaders than the ability to give orders. He found a common quality among most successful business leaders – an ability to outline a vision. The 'vision thing' has been an essential ingredient in business leadership ever since. Today, however, we can add emotional intelligence and that other variable, the ability to think strategically.

Strategy, vision and empathy mixed with some communication skills, a sprinkling of charisma – no longer considered essential but it still helps – and we're getting close. Add some know how (surprisingly this is still important), political skills, some luck, and a bit of presence (we might define this as glow – that special something that gets you noticed) and you're there. Of course it is almost essential to be male and it helps, also, to be tall and good looking, although there are plenty of exceptions. Just look at Bill Gates.

Leadership, then, is something more than being the boss. In fact you might be a boss and yet a hopeless leader – not so uncommon. You might be a leader on one occasion and follower on another. This is getting close to the Bennis definition, some reason why some linguistically challenged types in the US have written about 'followership'.

Sparkle and charisma

A true leader, however, knows when to lead and when to follow – yes, there's an answer for everything. Some may prefer to be agents of influence, some may be administrators or organisational wizards, some may have sparkle and charisma seeping from every pore. It's important to know, therefore, your leadership style, particularly if you are considering a career in a big company management where certain styles persist and where management structures incorporating staff appraisals, budgeting, cost centres and constantly changing demands are an ever present feature of the business.

At FTCareerPoint we don't pretend to have cornered the market in management development or even personal development, but we are trying to focus on career development, offering some simple on-site tools to help you analyse yourself. The leadership test, by Oxford Psychologists Press, one of the UK's leading test publishers is designed to add something to your insight.

Weakest link

The more you know about yourself, the more it is likely to confirm your style. It does not say, after completion, anything like 'you are the perfect leader', or, for that matter, 'you are the weakest link, goodbye', because, as we've seen, the demands of leadership differ for different circumstances. There are indeed times when you might need to give the order – 'do this and do it now', and make it stick. On other occasions there may be room for debate and consultation. This comes down to judgement, awareness and common sense (other good leadership qualities).

If you're up for it you could do the whole package of tests – leadership, emotional intelligence and personal values- found in the develop yourself section behind the blue door marked your career. Read the analysis carefully. The value is in the interpretation of the results and that extra understanding you may gain, however small, about your approach. In other parts of FT CareerPoint you can read some views of personality testing or psychometrics and on the thinking behind emotional intelligence.

This is a new web site and we're excited about its potential. With your help – we see this site as a community of interest (you can contribute to any of our discussion groups or suggest a new topic if you wish) – we aim to develop your own personality that can add real value to the business world that we inhabit.

Copyright © FT CareerPoint 2001. Reproduced with permission.

Questions for discussion

1   The article suggests that 'we're all managers now', whatever our level in the organisation. How realistic is this?

2   The article also suggests that in today's climate it is acceptable to challenge the most senior people. If we accept that this is a good thing, how can it be encouraged?

Activity

Access the leadership test provided on the *Financial Times* CareerPoint website at news.ftcom/FTCareerPoint/OPPQuiz. Complete the test to discover your strengths and weaknesses. Then design a development programme to address your key weakness.

See Chapter 26 for a framework to help you design such a development plan.

Feedback

1   *The article suggests that 'we're all managers now', whatever our level in the organisation. How realistic is this?*

Students may identify organisations that expect all individuals to take on managerial tasks (due to empowerment, teamwork and so on), and in addition they may cite the ways in which employers expect employees to take charge of their own development, and the reasons for this.

On the other hand we need to question whether all employees are capable of, interested in or willing to take this on – it may depend on their previous job experiences, abilities, life values and so on. What is needed to get people on board? Training, more pay for doing more, promotion opportunities?

2 *The article also suggests that in today's climate it is acceptable to challenge the most senior people. If we accept that this is a good thing, how can it be encouraged?*

For leaders students may suggest:

- Develop leaders so that they can accept criticism and deal with challenges in a constructive manner.

- Develop leaders to ask more questions of those who work for them.

- Develop leaders to realise that they don't have all the answers.

- Encourage leaders to provide appropriate forums to gather feedback.

- Develop leaders' emotional intelligence (could develop the detail of this).

- Leaders need to create an environment of trust.

For others students may suggest:

- Develop the confidence of others to contribute and challenge.

- Explore the nature of the roles of leaders and others.

- Promote those who challenge in a constructive manner.

- Might reward play a role?

CHAPTER 21 DIVERSITY: THE LEGAL FRAMEWORK

For the fifth edition we have divided the material on equality and diversity into two chapters. The first (Chapter 21) focuses on discrimination law in its different forms, the second (Chapter 22) on the other aspects of managing equality issues. In Chapter 21 we look in turn at each of the main areas which is currently covered by some form of anti-discrimination legislation. We start with sex discrimination, moving on in turn to discuss race discrimination, disability discrimination, discrimination for trade union reasons and that against part-time workers and ex-offenders. Many of the general concepts (direct and indirect forms, positive discrimination, harassment, etc.) are explained under the heading of sex discrimination, but are then referred to later in different contexts.

Additional teaching material

Here are some short case scenarios for students to read and consider. Each raises one or more important legal issues in the field of discrimination. They will find it helpful to refer to the relevant sections of Chapter 21 when thinking about each situation. Specific questions and/or activities are provided after each scenario has been described, together with lecturer feedback.

Case 21.1

The following job advertisement appears in a local newspaper:

Chauffeur Required
(£10,000 p.a.)

Safe and Sound Ltd is looking for a new chauffeur to undertake general driving duties on behalf of their Managing Director. Full clean UK driving licence essential. The successful candidate will have several years' experience in a similar role and will have an impeccable sickness record. He will have a pleasant manner and will be between 20 and 30 years of age. Hours of work are 7 am to 1.00 pm and 4.00 pm to 8.00 pm (Monday to Thursday). A smart, clean-shaven appearance and a high standard of spoken English are requirements of the role.

Please call 0161 111 2233 for further information.

In what different ways might this advertisement be in breach of employment law? Were you asked to give advice to the organisation concerned, how would you suggest that it was re-drafted to ensure that it complied with all legal requirements?

Case 21.2

You work as a personnel officer at a local authity's offices. A senior line manager called John Fraser comes to see you to ask your advice. Last week he interviewed a series of candidates for the position of departmental secretary. The role involves undertaking a range of administrative duties. It is full-time and requires the job-holder to work normal office hours. A pleasant and competent young woman aged 20 has been appointed.

One of the candidates, Fiona Pitt, was turned down despite having ten years' experience in a similar role with a neighbouring authority. One of the reasons for her failure to be selected was the receipt of a reference from her existing employer indicating a poor absence record. When asked about this at the interview she had talked about having suffered from a serious depressive illness over some months. According to her account, however, she was now receiving treatment for her condition and expected to be able to work normally. John Fraser tells you that he has now received a letter from Fiona Pitt claiming that in not appointing her the local authority is in breach of the Disability Discrimination Act 1995 (DDA). It is clear that she is considering legal action.

What general advice would you give John Fraser concerning this case? What further information would you want to know before recommending a course of action?

Case 21.3

The following email is sent to all female employees working in a local authority's offices by its equal opportunities officer:

> *Do you want to develop your career?*
>
> *Would you like to learn how to play the games men play to help them get on at work?*
>
> *If the answer is YES, you should apply for a place on our new career guidance course designed especially for women employed at Southington City Council.*
>
> *For further information call Sophie Smith on ext. 3456.*

The email is advertising a course designed by the training department to assist women with senior management potential. At present, although a clear majority of the council's employees are female, there are only a handful who have been promoted into management grades. All the most senior officers in the authority are men.

What legal risks are being run by Southington City Council in developing and publicising this training course? What changes would you recommend to ensure that the initiative met as many of its objectives as possible without breaching the law?

Case 21.4

Assume that you are employed as a human resources manager in a large firm of accountants. On the first day that the office reopens after the Christmas break you are approached by a secretary employed by the firm called Eva Rose. She is in a state of some distress and clearly fears the possible consequences of bringing her complaint to you.

Eva tells you that in the week before Christmas her department took an afternoon off work to attend a festive lunch at a nearby hotel. About thirty people were present, including two of the firm's senior partners (both men). Much drink was consumed, after which it was decided to play a series of party games. These became progressively more raucous as the afternoon went on. One game required participants to read poems out loud within a set time limit without hesitating or tripping over their words. When someone failed to achieve this they were required to pay a forfeit. Several of the poems had a sexual content and contained offensive language. When Eva was unable to read her poem out at the required speed, her forfeit was to sit on the lap of one of the senior partners for fifteen minutes. She had agreed to do this but says that she felt very uncomfortable doing so. After a short time she had left the party and had gone home.

Having told you about these events, Eva says that she has felt nervous about returning to work throughout the Christmas period. Now that she has arrived back she finds herself unable to concentrate because she is so embarrassed about what happened at the Christmas party.

What potential legal issues are raised by this case? What course of action would you take and why?

Feedback

Case 21.1

The main points students should make are as follows:

- Direct discrimination in using 'he' rather than 'they' or 'he/she'.

- Potential indirect discrimination in the age range specified, the hours (both on grounds of sex), the English requirement and the 'clean shaven appearance' (both on grounds of race) – none of which could be readily justified in the case of this job.

- The sickness record suggests an intention to discriminate against someone who is disabled or has been disabled for a period in the past – would be unlawful if this was taken into account at the shortlisting stage.

Case 21.2

The main points students should make are as follows:

- There would appear to have been a breach of the DDA here.

- Further investigation needed to establish whether the illness was the reason for the failure to recruit Ms Pitt:

  - If the answer is no, the authority may be able to defend itself at tribunal.

  - If the answer is yes, the authority should accept its mistake and seek an out-of-court settlement OR find an equivalent position for Ms Pitt (taking into account the requirement to make reasonable adjustments to accommodate her).

Case 21.3

The main points students should make are as follows:

- This is a case of positive discrimination, which is currently unlawful.

- The email needs to be redrafted so that it falls into the category of 'positive action', stopping short of actual discrimination on grounds of sex.

- Redrafting is necessary to take out references to men and women.

- A phrase could be inserted stating that women, because they are underrepresented at senior levels, are particularly encouraged to apply.

- The email needs to be sent to all staff (not just women).

Case 21.4

The main points students should make are as follows:

- This is clearly a potential case of sexual harassment.

- Any tribunal case could be brought against the employer, rather than the 'harassers', using the doctrine of vicarious liability.

- This is a form of direct discrimination, but one which allows the employer some defences

- The significant issue is whether or not there was perceived harassment on the part of the victim.

- The need now is to undertake a full investigation, and if necessary either formally or informally warn the individuals concerned.

- An alternative job should be provided for Ms Rose if practicable or desired by her.

- A harassment policy should be drawn up and circulated to all staff.

CHAPTER 22 EQUALITY: EQUAL OPPORTUNITIES AND DIVERSITY

This chapter is divided into three major sections. The first considers the current situation in employment terms for five defined minority groups based on gender, race, disability, age and sexual orientation. We establish that in spite of the equal opportunities legislation described in Chapter 21, there continues to be a differential employment experience for each of these groups, as compared with a young white heterosexual male with no disabilities.

The second part of the chapter assesses the two main approaches to resolving this difference – the traditional equal opportunities approach and the more recent management of diversity approach. We consider the fundamental assumptions underlying each approach and critique these and the impact of each approach. Our conclusion is that both approaches have something to offer (as well as blind spots) and that to abandon one in favour of the other would lead to missed opportunities. The final part of the chapter reviews applications of these equality approaches in different organisations.

Additional teaching material

The following article is published on the *Financial Times* CareerPoint website. It focuses on the issue of ethnic minority recruitment by universities. The article is concerned with developments in the United States, but the issues are as relevant and topical in the UK. Discussion questions and lecturer feedback are provided at the end.

A greater emphasis on diversity

By Betty Liu , *Financial Times* CareerPoint website, 10 August 2001

As efforts to end university affirmative action programmes – that is, positive discrimination – increase in the US, a peculiar trend is emerging: ever more aggressive minority recruitment. Nowhere is that more evident than at graduate business schools, where the perceived lack of concern about diversity has arguably the greatest impact – in the corporate arena. Minority enrolment in MBA programmes has always been small – about 15 per cent of all MBA students in the US. Black and Hispanic executives often complain of not feeling 'openly welcomed' at top business schools where it is not uncommon to see only a handful of minorities in a class of 300.

'Too many schools and too many MBA programmes have this elitist mentality – if students want to come here, they can apply,' says Henry Hernandez, a founder of the National Society of Hispanic MBAs. 'By doing that, you automatically talk to a smaller pool of candidates. The university becomes less accessible.' That is quickly changing as graduate business schools, eager to enlarge their student bodies and to entice corporate recruiters, intensify their search for minority applicants. In many ways, the banishment of graduate affirmative action programmes at universities in Texas, Florida and Michigan has only served as a wake-up call to administrators.

Leadership forums

'We had to find other ways to deal with the situation . . . so we began to work with [minority MBA associations] to sponsor leadership forums and to try to create an environment where minority students feel comfortable doing their MBA work,' says Gilbert Whitaker, dean of Rice University's Jesse H. Jones Graduate School of Management. In the past year, Florida State University's business school increased its advertising to attract more minority candidates; other state universities are offering aggressive race-based scholarships. The Jesse Jones School, in Houston, has attracted particular attention for its strong focus on increasing diversity. Much of that is attributed to Prof. Whitaker, who made diversity one of his chief priorities before taking the dean's position in 1997. During the past few years, the school has jointly held leadership seminars with the local chapters of the National Black MBA Association and the National Society of Hispanic MBAs. This month, more than 300 people are expected to attend the Hispanic forum, with panels discussing such topics as 'Entrepreneurship' and 'You as a brand'. Such projects have helped change the school's previous lofty, inaccessible image.

'Because Rice was viewed as an Ivy League-type school, people weren't very familiar with what it had to offer,' says Eric Lyons, president of the Houston black association chapter. The number of minority MBA students has grown from about zero four years ago to about 15 per cent this year. 'I'd like to see it closer to 20–25 per cent. Houston is about a third white, a third black and a third Hispanic,' says Prof. Whitaker. 'When I got here in 1997, there was one minority student out of 225. We're much better off than we were before, but we still have a lot we could do.'

Diversity

Prof. Whitaker was recruited because he engineered the same diversity changes at the University of Michigan's Business School, where he was also dean. 'The big pay-off was for everybody – the more diverse students we had, the more companies came to recruit and the bigger the applicant pool became.

'There's a direct correlation between the number of minorities in your student body and the number of companies eager to recruit,' he continues. 'In my time at Michigan, minorities went from three to 19–20 per cent of the student body and the number of companies recruiting went from 150 to 400.'

Corporations too are under pressure to diversify their management ranks. Last year, Coca-Cola settled a high-profile lawsuit alleging racial discrimination within the drinks group, a case that highlighted how the best companies may still fail to promote diversity. At the Jesse Jones School, the one-day seminars are sponsored by some of the biggest Fortune 500 companies – Shell Oil, Microsoft and Exxon Mobil – all of which are increasing their attempts at diversity. But the lack of minorities in MBA programmes is not always the fault of the university. Experts say young minority executives are not as inclined to enrol in MBA schools because they have not been coached to do so.

'Many times, those [minority members] who have graduated college may be the first ones in their family to obtain a degree. They may not necessarily have the knowledge or experience that says: "In order for you to advance, to get to the next level in your career, you have to continue your education,"' says Mr Hernandez. 'I was the first one in my family to get an engineering degree. I was mentored to think beyond just getting a bachelor's degree and to go on for a master's. But many people haven't been mentored like that.' Groups such as the Consortium for Graduate Study have tried to increase the number of minority applicants by offering MBA fellowships at participating universities. Yet much of the burden lies with the universities themselves and their local recruiting efforts.

The Hispanic and black associations note that the Jesse Jones School serves as a model for how a once lily-white MBA programme can be diversified in a meaningful way in a few years. 'We thought if Rice was going to be a great university and ... a business school, it ought to be a great one. Otherwise, better to use the resources for something else,' says Prof. Whitaker. He adds that it had been a vital element to increase student numbers.

Copyright © FT CareerPoint 2001. Reproduced with permission.

Questions for discussion

1   What methods identified in the article can be used to encourage non-white applicants on to MBAs?

2   How appropriate might these methods be for UK educational and professional bodies?

3   What is the value, in terms of equalising eventual employment experiences, of focusing on diversity in educational institutions?

4   What is the business case cited in this article?

Feedback

1   *What methods identified in the article can be used to encourage non-white applicants on to MBAs?*

The following may be identified:

- Working with minority MBA associations.

- To sponsor leadership forums/seminars.

- To try and change the lofty, inaccessible image.

- To try and create an environment where minority students feel comfortable.

- Race-based scholarships.

- Increased advertising.

2   *How appropriate might these methods be for UK educational and professional bodies?*

Probably it might be more difficult to find minority associations, but it just requires extra effort. Associations may be differently constructed. Could consider high-status universities, e.g. Oxford and Cambridge, and what would be appropriate for them. But what about professional associations in the area of accountancy, management, HR? How open would these associations be to this type of activity? What have these associations done so far and how effective has it been?

3   *What is the value, in terms of equalising eventual employment experiences, of focusing on diversity in educational institutions?*

Arguments may centre around enabling the students to gain necessary qualifications for higher level or specialist jobs. Such qualifications could engender higher levels of confidence, and also encourage individuals to apply for more senior jobs. However it may be argued that in spite of appropriate qualifications the other factors operating in these situations will stop individuals progressing.

4   *What is the business case cited in this article?*

The article suggests that focusing on minority students will enable universities to increase their headcount. This in turn, it is argued, also attracts higher numbers of potential employers to visit the students on the programme. In turn this encourages other students, of any race, to wish to join the programme in question.

CHAPTER 23 INTERACTIVE SKILL: THE APPRAISAL INTERVIEW

This chapter provides a general introduction to the practice of appraisal interviewing, taking a very practical perspective. Different types of interview and question are described, and suggestions are made as to what structure and general approach to take.

Additional teaching material

Below are several suggested class activities and discussion points.

1   The first page of Chapter 23 poses the question, 'Why persist with something that Tom Peters regards as downright dangerous?' The suggested answer is, 'we all seek approval and confirmation that we are doing the right thing, and most of us yearn to advise or direct what other people should do.' Is that an acceptable answer to the group?

2   How accurate and realistic does the group consider the categorisation of the management control approach and the development approach to be?

3   Run Activity 23.2 as buzz groups. Some appropriate jobs could be health visitors, teachers or police officers operating in areas with different levels of social deprivation or advantage. Alternatively sales representatives, some of whom are tasked to sell slow-moving items while others are selling more popular lines.

4   Run both practical exercises set out below. They do need to be done together. If necessary ignore items (a) – (c) above and go straight to the exercises.

5   How has doing the exercises helped members of the group to appreciate better the problems of performance management?

Practical exercises in appraisal interviewing

As with the exercises for Chapter 15, you need a very good friend to work with, but it is best if this person is someone with a job that they can talk through, so that there are real issues of concern that provide real value to the person from the discussion.

You take it in turns to interview each other. The aim is to talk real stuff about your respective jobs. One of you is A, the other is B.

First exercise 23.1

Preparation by A

Write down the response to the following questions on separate cards or pieces of paper:

(a)   An activity you perform in your job that is very important (this should begin with a verb, e.g. 'carrying out appraisal interviews', not a role or responsibility).

    (b)   An activity you do frequently – not necessarily important, but one which occupies a good deal of time.

    (c)   An activity, though important, unlikely to appear in your diary.

    (d)   What is the most important activity not so far listed?

Interview/discussion led by B on above topics:

    (i)   How are (a) and (b) similar, and how are they different?

    (ii)   What makes them easier, or harder, to do than (c)?

    (iii)   Which is it more important in your job to do well, (b) or (c)?

    (iv)   On what criteria did you select (d)?

    (v)   Which gives you most satisfaction, (a), (b), (c) or (d)?

Now change roles.

Exercise 23.2

Having begun the process of examining what you do with a colleague, you now move on to a similar exercise in which you have a different type of structure. It is a mini-appraisal in which you interview each other about work done in the first week of the month.

1   A interviews B for information about A's week. (15 minutes)

2   B interviews A for information about B's week. (15 minutes)

3   A and B prepare for feedback and discussion. (15 minutes)

4   B conducts appraisal interview with A about the week. (30+ minutes)

5   A conducts appraisal interview with B about the week. (30+ minutes)

6   A and B discuss with each other what they liked and disliked about the process.

Points to remember

- The first interview is for information gathering.

- The second interview is for feedback. This should include opportunities for positive reinforcement. Only criticise with care.

- A final discussion could consider the question: 'How useful did you find it to discuss an aspect of your work with someone who was well informed, but not your "boss"? Would it have been more or less useful having that discussion with your boss?'

PART IV CASE STUDY FEEDBACK

1   Some of the problems include:

(a) Lack of communication with, and preparation of, staff.

(b) Lack of clarity with the approaches adopted – should the systems tie together?

(c) An inconsistent approach adopted across departments.

(d) Lack of training of HoDs in objective setting and appraisal skills.

(e) Timescale.

(f) Lack of encouragement/opportunity for HoDs to get together and debate the ways the schemes should be implemented.

(g) Lack of understanding of the perceptions of staff.

2 & 3 For next year there is always the option of doing nothing and hoping that things will have settled down. Alternatively a combination of some of the following options could be used:

(a) Intensive communications campaign with staff to put across the aims and benefits of the schemes and how they will operate.

(b) An attitude survey to find out how staff really feel.

(c) A process to involve HoDs to discuss whether to link performance appraisal and PRP– a link may be agreed or alternative criteria for PRP involving part PA results plus other factors, including the possibility of peer review.

(d) Stating openly the criteria used for PRP once they have been decided.

(e) Discuss with HoDs whether to base PRP money on the team/department rather than the individual.

(f) Training for HoDs on objective setting and performance appraisal skills.

(g) Use the PRP money in alternative ways – involve staff in the decision – e.g. for conference visits, research funds, books, better departmental facilities, etc.

CHAPTER 24 STRATEGIC ASPECTS OF DEVELOPMENT

In this chapter we consider the difficulties of establishing the direct impact of investment in training and development on the overall performance of the organisation. In spite of this we argue that a strategic approach to training, learning and development is essential in today's climate in order to develop core competencies and competitive edge. We review different ways in which the link between training/learning/development strategy and organisational strategy can be viewed and review the characteristics of a strategic approach. We consider the impact of the external environment on a strategic approach and consider integration with other aspects of HRM. The stakeholders in training and development are explored together with different types of training and development roles. Finally we briefly comment on recent national initiatives.

Additional teaching material

The following article describes a new qualification launched by the Institute of Directors, enabling people to become Chartered Directors. Discussion questions and tutor feedback are provided at the end.

Certainly not a soft option

By Michael Skapinker, FT CareerPoint website, 22 June 2001

There are several senior positions you can hold without any formal qualifications – senior manager, parent and prime minister, for example. You can also be a company director without undergoing any real training.

In the UK, however, a growing number of senior executives are submitting themselves to an exhausting and rigorous process which allows them to call themselves chartered directors. The Institute of Directors, which has devised the chartered directors' programme, believes it is the first such qualification in the world.

It was formally launched just over a year ago, and 41 people have so far won the right to append the letters C.Dir. after their names. A further 60 directors have largely completed the process and up to 600 have passed the examination which would allow them to go on to the next stage. Other countries have expressed an interest in setting up something similar, although as the 'chartered' title is a peculiarly British phenomenon, only South Africa is considering following it this precisely. There have been approaches, however, from Scandinavia and Japan about incorporating parts of the process in a local directors' education programme.

Prerequisites

What does becoming a chartered director involve? You need to be at least 28 to begin the journey towards the qualification and you have to be a member or fellow of the IoD. You have to have been a company director for at least three of the previous five years.

You need a degree from a university or college acceptable to the IoD or have been admitted as a member of a profession recognised by the European Union. Not satisfying one of the latter two criteria is not fatal. You can still put yourself forward if you can demonstrate substantial experience; you have to have been a director in at least seven of the previous nine years. But the IoD insists that no more than 5 per cent of the total number of chartered directors are permitted to be degree-less. If there is a danger that the 5 per cent limit may be breached, you will be placed on a waiting list.

If you can scramble over all those hurdles, the hard work begins. First, to the undoubted distress of those who hoped they would never have to undergo such an experience again, there is an examination. The exam covers the director's role, finance, marketing, human resources, strategy and improving business performance.

The examination is followed by a review of the applicant's professional background. Candidates have to submit a self-evaluation of their experience as directors, along with a report by a colleague. Next comes one of the most gruelling parts: a personal interview by two senior members of the IoD.

After being approved by the interviewers, candidates have to agree to adhere to the IoD's code of professional conduct. This requires directors to serve the legitimate interests of the company's shareholders, exercise responsibility towards other stakeholders, refrain from anti-competitive practices and avoid conflicts of interest.

They also have to ensure that they do not 'recklessly or maliciously injure the professional reputation' of another member of the IoD. And they must agree to commit themselves to at least 30 hours of further continuing professional development each year.

Continuing development

Only after satisfying all those requirements do you have the right to call yourself C.Dir. Even then, there is no resting on your laurels. The continuing development programme is taken seriously. Chartered directors have to record their ongoing development on a 'record card', which must be produced on request.

The chartered director qualification is clearly no soft option. It is not the sort of process that every company director will feel able to endure. Tony Newton, the IoD's professional standards director, agrees. 'We've never seen this as something that would produce a mass market,' he says. 'It's quite time-consuming to do it. If you were to do it from a standing start, it would take you a year, probably more.'

There is no legal requirement for directors to obtain a qualification of this sort, so what are the advantages? It may make it easier to persuade investors or lenders that you are the sort of person to whom they should entrust their money, the IoD says. 'Chartered directors are likely to inspire greater confidence in their companies' banks, investors, suppliers and customers by providing additional evidence that their board operates with high professional standards and integrity,' the IoD says.

Learning experience

So, by granting the chartered director qualification, is the IoD providing holders with some sort of stamp of approval on which investors and lenders can rely? 'We've never suggested it was a stamp of approval,' Mr Newton says. What it shows is that the holder has invested a great deal of time in winning the qualification, has acquired substantial knowledge in the process and has committed himself or herself to a rigorous code of conduct.

What has the IoD learnt from the the first year of the qualification? First, that the paperwork was too onerous, Mr Newton says. It has been simplified. Second, that it is not just private sector directors who are interested in the qualification.

'We've been very interested to see how much people in the public and voluntary sectors have comparable requirements,' Mr Newton says. Leaders of charities and public sector bodies have been asking to qualify as chartered directors and Mr Newton says the IoD has been trying to ensure that the examination and interviewing process meets their needs too.

But is the chartered director qualification any guarantee of a company's commercial success? Does it ensure that a hospital or civil service department will work more efficiently or that a charity will be able to raise more money? Mr Newton agrees it does not. 'Nor did we ever seek to make it so. What is does provide is a guarantee that these people know what they ought to know and can be expected to behave in a professional way,' he says.

Copyright © FT CareerPoint 2001. Reproduced with permission.

Discussion questions

1   From a national perspective what is the advantage of the development and implementation of the qualification described in the article?

2   What are the perceived advantages of this qualification from the point of view of the directors and their organisations, as outlined in the article?

3   How appropriate are the processes that these directors have to go through to secure their qualification?

Feedback

1   *From a national perspective what is the advantage of the development and implementation of this qualification?*

Students may cite:

- Enhanced view of the quality of our industry leaders.

- Enhanced view of the importance we as a nation attach to training (may have knock-on effects) especially as we are at the leading edge of this.

- Role we might play developing the qualification elsewhere gives focus to UK training and expertise in this area.

- In a practical sense may improve the quality of our directors, therefore may improve business.

- The code of conduct may improve ethical business conduct across the UK

2 *What are the perceived advantages of this qualification from the point of view of the directors and their organisations, as outlined in the article?*

The article suggests that such directors are likely to inspire greater confidence from a range of sources – banks, investors, suppliers, customers, as the qualification indicates high standards. Could debate the implications of this. The knowledge requirements may improve actual performance.

3 *How appropriate are the processes that these directors have to go through to secure their qualification?*

Could be a range of issues to discuss here, e.g. the initial hurdles as well as the actual qualification. Debate could centre on the importance of self-analysis, the use of an examination, emphasis on continuous development, time commitment. For each of these issues, and others that are identified, the key question is whether the student can back up their case about appropriateness with reasoned argument.

CHAPTER 25 COMPETENCIES, COMPETENCE AND NVQs

We begin this chapter by noting the changing emphasis from academic education towards a more vocational approach, and identify the government's influence on this. The key message of the chapter is the difference between behavioural competencies and functional job competences (job standards as in NVQs), as these terms are often used very haphazardly, confusing the reader. We consider each approach in turn and give examples to demonstrate the nature of the approach. We outline usefulness, advantages and the problematic aspects of each approach.

Additional teaching material

The following article by Richard Donkin is a reminder of the concept of emotional intelligence which we first discussed in Chapter 20 on leadership. Student activities are suggested at the end.

Emotional intelligence

Review by Richard Donkin, FT CareerPoint website, 12 December 2000

In 1996 Daniel Goleman described a type of thinking called Emotional Intelligence in his book of the same name. The idea of emotional intelligence, as Goleman acknowledged, belongs to John Mayer, a psychologist at the University of New Hampshire, and Peter Salovey, of Yale University. Mayer defines emotional intelligence as 'the ability to perceive, to integrate, to understand and reflectively manage one's own and other people's feelings.' This seems to be suggesting that emotional intelligence demands qualities such as empathy and self awareness. A number of management consultancies, including Hay which has provided the test featured by FTCareerPoint, have decided that this kind of ability is just what is needed to run large companies, hence a whole new field of psychometric testing and leadership profiling.

Holistic approach

Goleman's book appeared at a time that many companies had undergone large cost-cutting and slimming down exercises partly in response to recession and partly inspired by the re-engineering theories of James Champy and Michael Hammer. Companies were looking for new leaders capable of delivering a more holistic approach to the way they ran business. These people would need the breadth of understanding to merge sometimes very different corporate cultures and workforces.

Whether or not, as some have suggested, emotional intelligence was no more than a clever form of branding for a thinking style that extended further than the merely analytical, Goleman's broader perspective of the qualities needed to succeed in life captured the public, but, more importantly, corporate mood. His first book, aimed mainly at parents, was quickly followed by another book, *Working with Emotional Intelligence*, directed at business.

Good at sums

The theories behind emotional intelligence stem from a conviction among some US psychologists that intelligence has been measured, in the past, too narrowly. The traditional measures awarded high scores to people with good memories or who were good at making calculations and analysing. But they did not, for example, measure empathy, common sense, motivation, persistence or social awareness.

Howard Gardner, the Harvard psychologist, speaks of 'multiple intelligences'. He lists seven different types. Another US academic, Robert Sternberg, professor of psychology and education at Yale University, lists three – analytical, practical and creative. Where they do agree is that this thing called intelligence is something more substantial than the ability to get all the questions right in the school exam.

Common sense

Emotional intelligence therefore, is perceived as more of a practical form of intelligence, combining qualities such as common sense and nous with inventiveness and worldliness. Perhaps it would have once been referred to as wisdom.

The emotional intelligence test you can undertake here, therefore, is not trying to measure your IQ. It is trying to assess a broader-based style of thinking. There are no right or wrong answers and a low score does not mean all is lost. Not all work requires vast amounts of empathy. But a low score might mean that you need to work on developing a more rounded approach to your job and to working with other people, particularly if the job involves managing people.

Crash landing

You might, for example, need to practice staying calm. As Daniel Goleman has pointed out, 'emotionally upset people cannot remember, attend, learn, or make decisions clearly.' In some ways it is easier to demonstrate where emotional intelligence is missing. Goleman uses the example of Melburn McBroom, a domineering, autocratic and temperamental boss who happened to be a pilot. He so intimidated his crew that when, on one flight, McBroom had a problem with landing gear, his crew were too afraid to tell him that the fuel was running out as the plane went into a holding pattern. It crashed, killing 10 people.

Daniel Goleman's personal definition of emotional intelligence relies on five components:

- Self-awareness – being in touch with our senses and feelings.

- Self-regulation – being in control of our emotions so that they do not interfere with the job.

- Motivation – the ability follow our desires and to persevere in the face of setbacks

- Empathy – sensing what others feel.

- Social skills – reading and dealing with relationships and emotional situations at work.

Look for evidence of your abilities in these areas in your individual responses to the *Emotional Intelligence* test questions.

Copyright © FT CareerPoint 2001. Reproduced with permission.

Note: the test referred to is a web-based test provided by HayGroup and is available via the *Financial Times* CareerPoint website. Should you wish to do the test there is no charge and the test results are returned immediately.

Activities

1   Log on to the FT CareerPoint website and answer the emotional intelligence question-naire. The address is www.ftcareerpoint.ft.com/ftcareerpoint. You then need to find the relevant link on the right-hand side of the screen under the heading 'Tools, Tables and Tests'.

2   Goleman's five components of emotional intelligence can be considered as five competencies. Write four behavioural statements against each of the five components.

Feedback

There are no right or wrong answers here. However, there are two tests to apply. First, the behavioural statement needs to relate to the competency in question, and second, it needs to describe behaviour that can be observed. The following ideas are a guide to the sort of answer that is expected:

Examples for Self-regulation

- Statement 1 – suggests 'time out' of a conversation when he/she is aware that they are becoming angry.

- Statement 2 – says things like 'this decision is not about our personal response, but about what's best for the business'.

Examples for Motivation

- Statement 1 – says things like 'we've gone too far with this one to give up now'.

Examples for Social skills

- Statement 1 – always involves new members or visitors in a conversation by asking them questions or addressing remarks to them.

CHAPTER 26 LEARNING AND DEVELOPMENT

We begin this chapter by considering the nature of learning and development, and we explore experiential learning, planned and emergent learning and learning curves. After this we offer a model of a systematic training and learning cycle, before we review different approaches to training and learning. We consider education and training courses, coaching, mentoring, peer support, action learning, self-development and open, distance and e-learning. We conclude with a brief review of evaluation approaches and methods.

Additional teaching material

Below are two articles looking at different ways in which new technology can be used in learning and development. In each case an activity or discussion question is provided, together with lecturer feedback. Both articles are published on the *Financial Times* CareerPoint website.

Article 26.1

An attraction based on similarities

By Della Bradshaw, FT CareerPoint website, 21 May 2001

Last month a group of professors from the Johnson School of Management at Cornell University headed north of the border to teach in a one-week programme on leadership at the Queen's School of Business in Kingston, Ontario. Unremarkable, you may think. But these professors were just the advance guard. Over the next few months, faculty from the two schools will be working increasingly closely to develop a partnership between the schools that could result in a full-blown alliance.

While schools such as Insead and the Wharton School at the University of Pennsylvania, and London Business School and Columbia in New York, announced their liaisons with a flourish of stage-managed hype, Queen's and Cornell have been more thoughtful and certainly more cautious in revealing their plans. Robert Swieringa, dean of the Johnson School, describes himself as optimistic about the alliance. 'We're trying to do this in a way that will make it work out,' he says. The critical factor will be faculty relationships, he says.

Compatibility study

The initial approach came from Margot Northey, dean of Queen's. The two schools carried out a strategic study to assess the 'fit' of their faculties and a financial analysis of the proposals. Prof. Swieringa believes the two schools have a lot in common: two research universities with a full range of degrees to doctoral level. Queen's is even moving into a renovated building in 2002 that looks remarkably like Cornell's home Sage Hall, says Prof. Swieringa.

Eventually the two schools could offer an executive MBA together, pool resources on short programmes and have researchers and PhD students working together on research and teaching. All options are still open. 'We have a lot of fallbacks if we don't get to a full alliance,' says Prof. Swieringa.

The big attraction of Cornell to Queen's is its Ivy League status and high-level ranking. In programme terms the attraction of Queen's to Cornell is its flagship executive MBA programme, which is delivered across Canada using video-conferencing. Queen's is perhaps the only top-notch school to have delivered a degree programme synchronously using video-conferencing technology to several sites in several time zones. And – critically – it has made money out of it.

Video-conferencing delivery

Queen's rival, the Ivey School at the University of Western Ontario in London, Ontario, has now closed its doors on its video-conferencing degree because of the expense of keeping the equipment up to date. The Wharton School delivered a number of highly rated short programmes across the US using video-conferencing; but also pulled out because the demand did not support the cost.

Queen's has kept down the cost by using the video-conferencing suites of some of its largest clients, notably Bell Canada, International Business Machines and Lucent, rather than purchasing its own equipment as Ivey did. It has also refined the pedagogy continuously since its introduction in 1984, says Donald Nightingale, associate dean for executive and MBA programmes at Queen's. 'Queen's has taken seven years to get where it is today . . . The quality of what the student gets is dramatically different today from what it was when we started.'

It has not always been plain sailing, says Prof. Nightingale. 'We very nearly failed financially early on.' Now, he says, the critical mass – Queen's enrolled 92 students in the Toronto region alone this year – means 'the programme makes money, it's a major supporter of the school'. Prof. Swieringa says that when he saw the programme in action he was particularly impressed: 'It's the best product I've seen anywhere.' In particular he likes the boardroom arrangement, which brings together between five and eight participants in each video-conferencing room to work in a team. At any one time more than 50 boardrooms can be connected to the network in 25 cities – if a region lacks demand one year, that boardroom is dropped from the network.

Effective learning

Rather than deliver lengthy lectures, professors have to break their presentations every 20 minutes so students can have local discussions or ask questions, something they do by 'voting' – electronically raising their hands by using a hand-held device that is issued to each participant. Students report that the system enables them to ask each other questions during lecture time – an accountant on the team, for example, can help the others with a tricky bit of number-work. Prof. Nightingale reports that this method of teaching is extremely effective. 'Learning is fundamentally a social activity. There is support in the boardroom that there is not in the lecture theatre.' One of Queen's biggest clients, Nortel, carried out internal assessments of various MBAs and found that managers were more satisfied with executive MBAs based on video-conferencing than with more traditional, classroom-based teaching. On Nortel's measure, participants were found to have absorbed 20 per cent more content on the video-conferencing course.

Technical staff are visiting Cornell from Queen's to assess what the US university will need to link into the programme and Cornell professors are learning what it takes to be a star of the video screen. When a link is established next year, the first Cornell students to participate in the boardroom teaching are likely to be those from the school's full-time MBA.

New participants

If the link proves successful, other schools could also participate – in the past Queen's has run a boardroom in Bermuda as part of its programme. The two schools were looking at including Itesm in Mexico to give a Nafta-style programme but the cost of video-conferencing links in Mexico proved prohibitive.

A second option is to include a European school, probably a British one. Names mooted include the Said School at the University of Oxford and Warwick Business School. Impressive though the technology may be, the hours of study may prove prohibitive. While a typical Saturday for participants in Toronto involves starting classes at 9.30am and finishing at 5.30am, Saturday night out for participants in the UK would take on a new meaning – classes until 10.30pm.

Copyright © FT CareerPoint 2001. Reproduced with permission.

Activity

From the article, identify the key issues which need to be resolved in order to successfully implement video-conferencing on a world-wide basis.

Feedback

The following may be anticipated:

- Cost of keeping the equipment up to date.

- Possibility of using facilities from large corporations to keep costs down.

- Recruiting sufficient numbers to offset costs and make a profit.

- Making sure the pedagogy is constantly updated.

- Ensuring quality.

- How many sites are appropriate and of what size?

- How to implement across different time zones.

- How to stimulate interaction and make sure the social aspects of learning are not neglected.

Article 26.2

A bankrupt idea's great future

By Della Bradshaw, FT CareerPoint website, 29 May 2001

Pensare, the start-up e-learning company that developed the technology for the Duke MBA Cross-Continent programme, is winding down operations and has filed for protection from creditors under chapter 11 of the US federal bankruptcy laws.

The decision will send a shiver through the rest of the e-learning community, which has seen a squeeze on venture capital funding on the one hand and a decline in paying customers on the other. Pensare's demise will call into question many of the predictions made for the e-learning market. International Data Corporation, for example, estimates the global market for online learning will grow from $6.3bn (GBP4.5bn) to $23bn (GBP16bn) in 2004.

Pensare launched its latest technology, called P3, in August but then faced a funding squeeze, as did the rest of the dotcom community. Autumn saw a decline in customers, says Katharine Leary, chief executive of Pensare. 'It really tightened in January. None of us could have predicted how quickly the corporate market would close down.'

Duke Corporate Education, the for-profit arm of Duke University's Fuqua business school, is acquiring the assets and intellectual property rights surrounding the P3 platform, to develop it for its own use. Duke's students have transferred to the platform.

Pensare's demise is the latest in a series of setbacks for US e-learning companies. Quisic (formerly University Access), the California-based company seen as among the most active in the business school market, has pulled out of education almost entirely because of lack of funding. Instead of the long-term profits Quisic had hoped to make from the university segment, it is now playing for the quick buck by focusing on the corporate sector, in particular 25 core corporate clients. The plan is to be profitable by the year's end. 'It's a good discipline, getting to profitability quickly,' says Alec Hudnut, chief executive officer.

Quisic has closed its academic office with the loss of 60 jobs. Among the 60 was Chuck Hickman, long-time supremo at the AACSB, the American business school accreditation body and one of the best-known characters on the US business school scene. After losing his job at Quisic he began talks with Duke Corporate Education about an appointment there but changes of plan at Duke led to that job falling through before it had begun.

Mr Hickman is philosophical: 'This is dotcom life. We business schools teach this stuff but it doesn't mean we are very good at it.'

The implications of the Quisic retrenchment are being felt particularly strongly at London Business School and the Kenan-Flagler school at the University of North Carolina at Chapel Hill. Quisic had a deal with LBS to develop half a dozen courses to be put online. Only one has been completed.

UNC had been planning to run an executive MBA programme for corporate clients supported by Quisic technology. That has now been shelved too and Kenan-Flagler is working on a new model for its EMBA, to be announced soon. The school says the downturn in the US economy also contributed to the withdrawal of the programme, which relied heavily on the corporate sponsorship of students.

The best-known company in the market, UNext, has also laid off staff but its chairman, Andrew Rosenfield, says this is because most of the technical development work is over. Unlike Pensare and Quisic, UNext (which used to be known as UNext.com – the .com suffix has been diplomatically dropped) has attracted more funding and some well known clients.

The most notable of these is General Motors, which will offer internet courses to all 88,000 of its employees. The deal will help GM contain costs, says Mr Rosenfield. 'They have a puzzle. In periods of pressure how [do they] cut costs without reducing the quality of the product?'

It will also swell UNext's coffers, as will the deal with Thomson, the media company. Thomson will invest $9m during each of the next four years in UNext, which works with top universities Chicago, Columbia, Stanford, Carnegie Mellon and the London School of Economics.

GM also received warrants as part of the deal that enables them to invest in UNext in due course. A fourth player in the market is FTKnowledge (part of the Pearson group, owners of the *Financial Times*). Managing Director Pippa Wickes says FTK has been moving away for some time from the stand alone e-learning products towards 'blended' offerings, combining face-to-face teaching and on-line learning. Such is the executive MBA that FTK will launch with the Judge Institute at Cambridge University and the course on managing people being developed with the University of Michigan. She predicts FTK will break even in 2002.

Mr Hudnut acknowledges that Quisic's entrance into the corporate market has increased its competition with UNext. 'I do think we are ending up more squarely in the same competitive arena,' says Mr Hudnut. 'I think the academic market is still a good market – in the long term.' Other big losers, in the short term at least, will be the business schools and universities that had the option of converting into equity the royalties from programmes sold. Only 18 months ago both Chicago and Columbia universities, the first to sign with UNext, estimated that they could each own up to 6 per cent of the company by converting royalties in this way. At that time the market valued a 6 per cent stake at anything up to $750m.

As to Pensare, the deal between it and Duke Corporate Learning should be concluded by the second week in June. The important question will be whether Duke, in essence a university and a content supplier, will have the resources to upgrade and to exploit the technology continuously as a commercial product. James Gray, associate dean at the Fuqua school, expresses few doubts. 'We think we have the best distributed learning platform in the world.'

Ms Leary is also confident the Pensare technology will be a winner in the long term. 'I still think it will revolutionise the way education will be done. But it will be under a different name, not Pensare.'

In spite of his present predicament Mr Hickman also believes e-learning has a strong future. 'I look at this market and I still believe the demand for e-learning will continue to grow in certain segments . . . but it is evolving more slowly than many of us could have guessed three years ago.'

Copyright © The Financial Times group 2001. Reproduced with permission.

Question for discussion

What issues need to be identified for the successful implementation of e-learning by educational providers?

Feedback

From the article the following issues may be identified:

- Take-up may grow much more slowly than anticipated.

- Software developers may suffer financial problems and withdraw.

- Universities/businesses may employ suppliers who do not fulfil their contracts to produce systems, or do this more slowly than anticipated.

- Funding and take-up will be affected by the external business climate.

- Do the content suppliers (i.e. universities) have the funds to develop robust systems?

- Is a combined approach (i.e. e-learning plus face-to-face learning) better (more popular) than a pure e-learning approach?

CHAPTER 27   CAREER DEVELOPMENT

In this chapter we first review how and why careers are changing and debate whether these changes are perceptions, or whether they reflect reality. We discuss in some detail the new psychological contract, comparing this to the old psychological contract, and we question the extent to which the new psychological contract is actually applied. From this we progress to define the nature of career development and recognise that in this chapter our perspective is that of the individual, rather than the perspective of the organisation which we took in Chapter 5. Different perspectives to understanding careers are discussed, for example career stages and Schein's career anchors. Finally we discuss the ways in which individuals can manage their careers and what support organisations and managers can provide.

Additional teaching material

The following article is published on the FT CareerPoint website. It describes the activities of careers consultancies in providing advice and finding opportunities for individuals. Discussion questions and feedback are provided at the end.

Agents for career change

By Alison Maitland, FTCareerPoint website, 9 May 2001

Phil Schneidermeyer is a 'chief talent scout' but his clients are not footballers or Hollywood hopefuls. He is one of a small but growing number of agents who manage the careers of high-flyers in the corporate world.

Mr Schneidermeyer left Korn/Ferry International, one of the world's largest executive search firms, last year to set up his Connecticut-based Talent Intelligence Agency, specialising in senior technology professionals.

The uncertain economic climate, with waves of job cuts being announced each week, may seem the obvious time for employees to make contingency plans. But career management has been growing during economic boom as well. The ill-fated leaps that many made to new jobs during the dotcom frenzy highlight the need for careful planning at all times.

'Executives are being a lot more proactive about their careers,' says Shannon Kelley, marketing director of the Association of Executive Search Consultants in New York. 'I think it's a mindset that's developing, independent of the economic cycle. People know companies won't necessarily be loyal and they also want a varied career, not necessarily within the same company.'

Mr Schneidermeyer says the jobs market is demanding a new model, 'one that puts the executive first while introducing him or her to a range of career opportunities and professional challenges'.

Career agent

Unusually for a career agent, he does not charge individual clients for advice, preferring to recoup his costs from the companies who recruit them. 'It's taking the idea of specialisation in executive search to the next level. We want to know these people now and for the long term.'

Given the economic downturn, he is advising clients with itchy feet 'to enjoy their present position for another six months and then look around'. But he does not appear unduly worried about business, arguing that software developers and their managers are among the least dispensable in any cuts.

Personal career agents target an exclusive clientele. The website of STI, a Californian executive management firm, boasts that it will 'define your personal brand vision' using consultants such as Richard Greene, presentation coach to the late Diana, Princess of Wales. But the emergence of such agents reflects a wider trend for professionals and managers to take control of their careers. 'There's a multiplicity of ways careers can happen,' says Maury Peiperl, director of the careers research initiative at London Business School. 'In recent history, we have gone from company man to empowered person.' Young high-flyers have different expectations of a career. 'If you talk to some of the new MBAs and the top university graduates, they're starting out thinking that they should do their own thing.'

What has caused this shift? The cuts that signalled the end of 'jobs for life' were not forgotten as the last recession gave way to economic growth. Nor did they end there. Redundancies continued throughout the upswing as companies merged, restructured and shed staff to meet changing needs. Not surprisingly, it became more acceptable for employees to move to a rival company or to start their own business.

The corporate response to these changes has been to sponsor career development and coaching for employees, particularly the most prized. In-house programmes have been the fastest-growing form of executive education in the past decade.

Recruitment and staffing agencies, in turn, have been expanding their range of 'human capital management' services. Last year, for example, Manpower bought a stake in SHL, the UK psychometric testing supplier. This year Whitehead Mann Group, the UK-based executive search firm, acquired The Change Partnership, a coaching company.

'There's increasing global competition and [corporate] clients are asking for more,' says Kevin McNair, a director of Granville Baird, an investment banking group that advises the 'human capital management' sector. 'What they've all been trying to do is become more important to the client.'

Moving on

But in-house career development programmes are limited in that they tend to assume employees will stay put. Who helps those who want to move on? In the past few years, most of the big executive search firms have launched online career management services aimed at individual candidates.

Futurestep.com was set up by Korn/Ferry in 1998 after a study by The Boston Consulting Group found that middle managers felt let down by recruitment agencies. 'There wasn't the same relationship as at senior levels,' explains Simon Wiggins, UK managing director of Futurestep. 'They felt they didn't get any help or value.'

The site, where registration is free, offers online self-assessment, information on leadership and communication styles, advice on the jobs candidates would be best suited for and an idea of their market worth.

Will search firms, established to serve employers, pay even greater attention to candidates' needs in future? Mr McNair is doubtful. 'These are relatively inexpensive feel-good practices that will hopefully keep candidates eye-balling their sites and in contact with them,' he says. 'Ultimately, their responsibility is to their clients and that's where they're going to spend their real money.'

Indeed, there is a fundamental conflict between the recruitment industry's imperative to fill vacancies and the needs of some candidates to take control of their careers by changing course. Prof. Peiperl says career management should start with individuals asking what drives them, what their ideal job would be, and which skills and relationships are most important to them. 'If you start with what's available, you limit yourself. The idea of fitting people into jobs is slowly shifting towards finding jobs to fit people.'

Individual potential

This is an appealing notion. But people who have been wedded to a single career might find the idea of breaking out on their own a little daunting. A new type of counselling agency, focusing on individual potential rather than labour market need, is emerging in response.

One example is New Directions, a Boston-based outplacement company which has set up a 'portfolio programme' for senior people who want a change from a traditional career. The mix of options on offer ranges from business and entrepreneurship to education, charitable work, 'spiritual' work, and leisure time, says Bill Reading, vice-president of marketing and sales. 'We find out what their personal interests are. We don't have an endgame when we start.' This is a service for older, well-heeled clients or for people whose companies are paying because they are being made redundant or taking early retirement: fees range from $8,000 (£5,500) to $35,000.

The fees charged by Careers by Design, a London-based agency, are more modest at £650–£1,500 and clients vary widely in age and background. Many are highly successful but feel something is missing in their lives, says Elizabeth Klyne, who founded the agency three-and-a-half years ago. 'There's an increasing unwillingness for people to sacrifice their whole life for the sake of their careers,' she says.

Her programmes aim to discover what each person has to offer – their 'unique contribution' – and what changes are needed to make this contribution a central part of their working lives. One former client is Phyllis Santa Maria, a 57-year-old consultant in electronic learning, who explains what this new approach to career development means to her. 'So often we live our lives in a big rush and just don't stop and listen,' she says. 'The question is not what am I doing in my career, but what am I doing in my life?'

Copyright © FT CareerPoint 2001. Reproduced with permission.

Questions for discussion

1   From the article identify the different roles that agencies may have in promoting the career development of individuals, particularly high-flyers.

2   What does the article suggest about how high-flyers are now managing their own careers?

Feedback

1   *From the article identify the different roles that agencies may have in promoting the career development of individuals, particularly high flyers.*

Students may suggest the following:

- Introducing a range of career opportunities and professional challenges outside their own organisation, often with no charge.

- Help individuals 'define their personal brand vision'.

- Coaching services for professionals.

- On-line career management services – e.g. free registration for self-assessment tools, information on leadership and communication styles, advice on the most suitable jobs and an idea of their market value.

- Helping individuals move away from a tradition career path – support them in understanding their values and interests. Usually charged.

- Career–life balance advice.

Ask students if they have ideas about how these services may be added to.

2   *What does the article suggest about how high fliers are now managing their own careers?*

It suggests they are looking for a varied career, not just with one company. It suggests they feel empowered and are less of a 'company person'. They are more proactive at managing their careers and will often move to a rival company or start their own business.

Could ask students to what extent this approach applies to the ordinary employee.

CHAPTER 28 INTERACTIVE SKILL: PRESENTATION AND TEACHING

In this practical, skills-oriented chapter we start by looking at different approaches to the learning process and at different types of learner. We go on to look at alternative approaches to instruction and to the making of presentations.

Additional teaching material

Here are five practical exercises in teaching and presentation to use in a classroom setting.

1   Devise a training programme that will teach someone to complete a straightforward task, taking care to go through all the steps of preparation that have been mentioned in this chapter. Then teach someone to complete the task.

Some of the tasks you could consider are:

- folding a table napkin;

- laying out a tray to serve someone a full English breakfast in bed;

- doing a conjuring trick;

- teaching the rudiments of sign language;

- making a cake;

- packing a collection of tinned food in a box;

- laying out a tray, as above, but for someone who is left-handed.

2   At a meeting you attend in the near future, identify which of the following impediments to constructive discussion and understanding or action were present:

- some people talking too much and others making no contribution;

- poor agenda or no agenda;

- poor chairing.

After the meeting try to work out what caused the problems, but think it through fully. For instance, did the people who talked too much do so because they thought it was expected of them, because they always talk too much, because they did not understand what was happening, or for some other reason?

How could these problems have been overcome?

Would you have been able to deal with them?

3   When attending a presentation or listening to a speech given by someone else, study the arrangement of the room and note the changes that you would (and could) make if you were the speaker. Why have you done that?

4   Obtain from your library a book or audio cassette of speeches made by an effective orator, such as Winston Churchill, Billy Graham, John Kennedy, Martin Luther King or a politician you approve of, and make notes of the plan of their material.

5   Prepare a five-minute speech on one of these topics:

     (a)   Music

     (b)   Health and fitness

     (c)   Your favourite sport

     (d)   Your hobby

     (e)   Your first boyfriend/girlfriend.

After preparation, deliver the speech in an empty room (the garage would do) and record (audio) it. Play it back several times, making critical notes of energy level, voice, pace, pauses, etc., following the points in the chapter, then deliver the speech again while making a recording.

- In what ways is it better?

- In what ways not as good?

- What have you learned about the way you speak?

- What can you still improve?

If you can move on to video-recording, the benefit of the exercise is greater, but it is wise to start with audio recording and probably better not to video-record for a wider audience than yourself. Group discussion of video-recorded presentations can be very inhibiting.

PART 5 CASE STUDY FEEDBACK

1 Immediate steps to help consultants are most likely to be in the area of training and personal development:

   (a) To strengthen selling and persuasion skills for those consultants who are less comfortable with this area.

   (b) To develop training skills in all consultants.

   (c) Some consultants may need support in handling stress.

   (d) Managers may need training and development in some of these areas, and in coaching and counselling skills to aid consultants.

   (e) Alternative careers may need to be sought internally or externally for those consultants who, after receiving support, still feel that they are mismatched to their jobs.

2 In the longer term the multiskilling goal may be met partly by careful future recruitment, and partly by long-term intensive training and development to build both skills and confidence.

   In respect of a career structure, there may be some scope for developing jobs that require multiple skills, but which have a distinct emphasis, so that consultants can be matched to jobs that contain a balance of tasks which are in line with their strengths. The company will also need to consider whether multiskilling is appropriate for all jobs. It could be appropriate to have a technical promotion ladder so that there is a reservoir of specialist expertise, which may be **technically** multiskilled and flexibly used.

   Outplacement schemes **may** be considered for a small number who are not comfortable with the new structure; or the company may wish to bide its time and wait for these individuals to leave of their own accord.

3 Reward strategy needs to support the development and use of multiple skills, and recruitment strategy needs to be used to attract and select those who are already multi-skilled or who have the potential to work in this way. A strategy to develop a culture which values multiskilling, continuous development and coaching/support of others may be appropriate.

4 This could be developed in-house or by bringing in a firm which specialises in competency development. As the new role is just being developed it would be difficult to develop the profile fully at this stage using the method adopted by Boyatzis, although this could be used at a later date to check that the profile was appropriate.

   An alternative may be to consult with managers regarding the competency profile and, for example, engage in brainstorming sessions, or discuss profiles used elsewhere in similar contexts. The Boyatzis method may be used to determine part of the profile relating to that part of the consultancy role which is already being carried out.

Once developed, the competency profile could be used for selection, assessment centres, development planning, performance planning and assessment, promotion decisions, and as a contribution to reward decisions.

CHAPTER 29 STRATEGIC ASPECTS OF EMPLOYEE RELATIONS

In Chapter 29 we look at the context for employee relations and at some of the alternative approaches that are available for organisations to take, given the constraints of the environment. We start with a brief historical survey, taking the reader from the nineteenth century to the present day. The purpose is to demonstrate how profoundly and rapidly the employee relations environment has changed in the past and may well change in the future. It also serves as a means of explaining the origins and evolution of the key employee relations institutions and traditions we observe in organisations today. This is followed by two sections looking, respectively, at the main forms of collective and individual employee involvement. The strengths and weaknesses of each, from a management perspective, are discussed; as well as day-to-day practical considerations. The chapter ends with a section drawing attention to the very varied context for employee relations that exists across national boundaries.

Additional teaching material

Exercise 29.1

In the following article, Robert Taylor assesses the likely future direction for trade unionism in the western industrialised economies. A union perspective is taken here, providing a different angle to that of Chapter 29. He concludes that the trade union role is probably going to be more rather than less marginal in the future than is currently the case. Discussion questions and lecturer feedback are provided at the end.

A bridge to work's future

By Robert Taylor, FT. com website, 20 August 2001

Next Monday is Labour Day in the US, almost officially recognised as the end of summer and the return to work. A week later the British Trades Union Congress gathers in Brighton for its annual conference in what marks the start of the new political season. The yearly ritual resumes with signs of apprehension about employment prospects across the western world. Do we face a slowdown or a full-blown economic recession? Financial markets, information technology companies, manufacturers, economists and analysts regale us with confused, conflicting prognoses.

But a return from the beaches provides an opportunity to look beyond the present moment to the future of employment. Think-tanks, research institutes and government-funded research examine and analyse the complexities. Where will the new jobs come from? What will be the relationship between companies and their employees? Are we going to experience a steady or dramatic growth in part-time, temporary limited contract employment at the expense of those permanent, full-time and secure jobs that we were accustomed to have in the decades after the Second World War?

Many of these questions are probably unanswerable on today's evidence. What seems clear is that we are involved in a long-term and fundamental transformation of employment relations.

The independent Economic and Social Research Council in the UK funds a wide-ranging research programme on the future of work.

The once seemingly settled world of negotiated national or industry-wide collective bargaining in the US, UK and elsewhere has either gone or nearly gone. The overwhelming majority of employees are no longer members of trade unions in many western economies. In the US private sector fewer than one in 10 workers is unionised. Nor is the picture different in much of Europe. We see the spread of individualised forms of wage negotiations and contract agreements at enterprise level no longer mediated or negotiated by trade unions but imposed by employers. It may be true that in the UK recently a significant number of employers has displayed greater readiness to negotiate with trade unions to promote workplace change by consent. Under the fashionable term of 'partnership', companies seek to improve productivity.

Trade unions in the UK and elsewhere in Europe are rebranding as allies in business-led innovation rather than as forces of resistance to change. This will not ensure a return of trade union power or a strengthening of the employee's bargaining position. But it suggests that non-unionism among employees will not necessarily mean a reassertion of unilateral employer authority.

Modernisation, work restructuring and job re-design are recasting shop-floor attitudes more positively and flexibly. So we see a shift from traditional forms of industrial relations based on voluntary accommodations and negotiated compromises with a recognised acceptance of differing interests towards a system that balances a partnership model with agreed concerns and employer acceptance of at least a basic framework of rights.

But determining the balance may arouse widespread debate. Employers are having to come to terms with what they often regard as time-consuming regulation imposed on them by the state. In regard to training, grievances and job losses, equal opportunities and work/life balance issues, for example, companies small and large find it necessary to establish formal procedures and rules.

Some unions are now offering their services to companies by agreeing to deal with those issues not in an adversarial manner but in a spirit of consensus. As service providers, mutual aid societies and learning organisations, trade unions are also considering how to raise the confidence of the employees they represent and improve their value in the eyes of employers. It is unclear whether most trade unions – formed decades ago – have the flexibility to respond. It is painfully clear, however, that trade unions and others are increasingly seen by many young people in western labour markets as backward-looking, middle-aged and male-dominated bodies. Unions tend to be concentrated in the public services sector among professionals with above-average earnings and job security, rather than in the ever-expanding, diverse private services that are the engines of employment growth.

It is not only in the US that private sector workplaces are becoming overwhelming union-free zones where fewer than one in 10 employees is unionised. In the UK, unions find it difficult to maintain a workplace presence. In sectors such as business and financial services, retailing, hotels and catering and small enterprises, trade unions seem almost extinct.

None of this reflects settled, trouble-free labour markets with satisfied employees. The evidence suggests that many employees on both sides of the Atlantic remain dissatisfied. They feel they lack the respect of their employer and they want their jobs to be more interesting. They want a say in controlling and shaping the work they do. They also want greater security. Many companies are having to introduce information and consultation arrangements to strengthen bonds of loyalty and commitment.

The recently agreed European Union directive on employee consultation and information rights may provide a way forward. But this seems more likely to come by using such regulation as a back-stop, paving the way to greater use of joint management–employee forums, established voluntarily. Mere existence of regulation can act as a stimulant for change by consent. But none of this promises an untroubled future. We are likely to see a wider variety of employee relationships. For those employees with marketable and transferable skills and highly rated formal qualifications, the outlook is promising, with sophisticated and flexible employment packages either in full-time jobs or on short-term contracts. But for those on the margins of the labour market moving in and out of low-paid, unskilled and insecure jobs, times may prove increasingly harsh and uncertain.

The decline of employee representation will drive the world of work in contradictory directions. We are not so much creating a new world of work as returning to something familiar to the 19th century – with one fundamental difference. In the days of iron and steel, coal and engineering and other bastions of industrialisation, labour was seen as a coherent, real and independent force in a world of class conflict. Next Monday's Labour Day – introduced in the US in 1894 in the aftermath of the Pullman strike – is a reminder of those times. But today's world is arguably much more complex and fragmented without substantial labour movements. Trade unions are in danger of becoming only repositories of memories.

This column is based on the author's Future of Employment Relations, *to be published next week by the Economic and Social Research Council's future of work programme.*

Questions for discussion

1   Make a list of the different factors you consider to be important in explaining the decline in trade union influence around the world. Which of these do you think is the most important factor?

2   Robert Taylor's article makes some suggestions about how trade unions might regain some influence in the workplace. How far are these likely to meet with success? What other approaches could trade unions try?

Feedback

1   *Make a list of the different factors you consider to be important in explaining the decline in trade union influence around the world. Which of these do you think is the most important factor?*

This is a big topic which has generated a great deal of excellent academic research in recent years. Most agree that various different factors are at play. Some of the more important are as follows:

- Growth in the percentage of employees working in the services sector combined with a decline in manufacturing employment.

- A period of relatively high unemployment.

- A period of relatively low price inflation.

- Development of more sophisticated human resource management practices (e.g. individual employee involvement).

- The evolution of employment law as an alternative source of protection.

- In some countries, government hostility towards trade unions.

- Poor media image of trade unions/perception of them as change resistors in 'opposition' to employers.

2   *Robert Taylor's article makes some suggestions about how trade unions might regain some influence in the workplace. How far are these likely to meet with success? What other approaches could trade unions try?*

The main alternative approaches (not necessarily mutually exclusive) are as follows:

- Campaign for a more favourable legislative environment.

- Improve relevance and image.

- Work with employers 'in partnership' rather than against them.

- Provide a greater range of services for members (e.g. legal advice, credit cards, crèches, insurance, leisure clubs, etc.).

Exercise 29.2

Suggested topic for a classroom debate:

> **Management/union conflict within an organisation should be reduced to the minimum as it is always harmful.**

> **Pro**

> Some regard conflict in organisations as inevitable because of the inescapable conflict of interest in the employment relationship, and not necessarily dysfunctional. Such views are betrayed by their age. They were put forward at a time of management uncertainty and

weakness in the face of growing trade union organisation and assertiveness. Unable to prevent the escalation of conflict between management and trade unions, managers looked for a rationalisation of their failure and academics complied by providing reassuring explanations. When Allan Flanders described unions as 'the opposition that could never become the government' he demonstrated the predominantly negative effect that union recognition has within an organisation. The only purpose of the union is to stop the management doing things. Sometimes it may stop the management from being foolish or unfair, but it will also delay necessary innovation by opposing initiatives that employees do not like, even though the dislike may be unreasonable, ill informed or chauvinistic. Union recognition acts as a brake on the growth and flexibility of an organisation, and undermines the confidence and authority of managers to take risks and make necessary decisions.

Con

Managers competing for business have to seek competitive advantage. When the quality or uniqueness of the product or service is not sufficient to maintain that advantage, they look for cost saving and flexibility in operations. That usually means disadvantaging the employees by limiting pay advances, resisting improvements in terms and conditions, redundancy, more onerous working conditions or general 'tightening up'. Apart from the impact on the rights and reasonable expectations of the employees themselves, these manoeuvres are usually in response to a crisis and the need to find short-term alleviation of a problem. Actions taken in such situations are frequently ill advised as the need to do *something* is greater than the need to do the *right thing*. Union resistance at this point will first of all protect employees against the effects of inadequate management decisions and – through approaching the problems from a different point of view – will force managers to review their decisions with the benefit of more consideration, especially of the long-term implications. Unions in the end are powerless to stop the management saying 'No', but their intervention can greatly improve the quality of management decisions.

CHAPTER 30 RECOGNITION AND CONSULTATION

This chapter starts by looking in more detail at the topic of trade union recognition. Whereas in the last chapter, and in Chapter 2, the general issue of the role played by trade unions was introduced, we turn here to the nitty gritty. We look at the recognition elements incorporated in the Employment Relations Act 1999, at different forms of union recognition and at derecognition situations. In the second half of the chapter the focus shifts to collective consultation. We summarise the areas in which there is now (at least in theory) a requirement on employers to carry out consultation with union representatives or via some other elected employee body. We also look at the practical reality of consultation exercises, at how they can 'go wrong' from a management point of view and at the role played by HR specialists in helping to ensure that they do not.

Additional teaching material

The following short *Financial Times* news article concerns the new EU Directive on information and consultation in the workplace. The Directive was finally accepted by the governments of each member state in June 2001 after years of hard negotiation. Originally the European Commission planned simply to extend the existing provisions for European Works Councils (described in Chapter 30) to all sizeable organisations. However, this plan was strongly resisted by the UK and Irish governments. A 'watered-down' compromise was eventually agreed to which all governments signed up, and it is this which is the focus of Brian Groom's article. Discussion questions and lecturer feedback are provided at the end.

NATIONAL NEWS: Drive planned to preserve compromise on worker rules

By Brian Groom, *Financial Times*, 2 August 2001

Britain is planning a 'charm offensive' this autumn to persuade the European Parliament not to undermine a delicate compromise on common rules for worker consultation across the European Union.

Alan Johnson, trade and industry minister, will visit MEPs in Brussels in an effort to prevent them from reversing concessions won when Britain agreed to the information and consultation directive in June.

After resisting the directive for months, Britain bowed to the inevitable at a meeting in Luxembourg after Germany, Ireland and Denmark's willingness to accept a deal meant being outvoted.

The directive provides for workers at companies with more than 50 employees within an individual member state to be consulted on decisions 'likely to lead to substantial changes in work organisation or in contractual relationships', such as redundancies or the sale of subsidiaries.

Britain agreed to the deal after securing phased implementation. When implemented in three years, it will apply only to companies with 150 or more staff, and after a further two years, to those with 100 or more staff. After seven years, it will apply to businesses with 50 or more workers.

The government fears MEPs, who must give the directive a second reading before it is approved by the council of ministers, may try to stipulate sanctions against companies that fail to comply. In the draft directive, this is left to member states.

EU employment ministers agreed in Luxembourg that member states must provide for 'appropriate measures in the event of non-compliance . . . in order to ensure that adequate administrative or judicial procedures are available to enable the obligations deriving from the directive to be enforced'.

They must provide for 'effective, proportionate and dissuasive' penalties if the directive is infringed.

Britain is supported by Belgium, the current holder of the EU presidency, which is pointing out to MEPs how difficult it was to achieve the compromise.

If the directive is approved, the government will face difficult talks with employers' organisations and trade unions about how it is to be implemented. Ministers are likely to seek as much consensus as possible.

The Luxembourg deal was criticised by the Confederation of British Industry, which said it was 'a step in the wrong direction that could undermine the ability of managers to manage'.

But John Monks, general secretary of the Trades Union Congress, said it was a 'breakthrough' and that for the first time employees in all the EU's medium and large companies would have the right to find out what their companies planned and to have their views heard.

Copyright © The Financial Times Limited 2001. Reproduced with permission.

Questions for discussion

1   Why do you think successive UK governments are so cautious about agreeing to measures of the kind found in this Directive and in the earlier one requiring 'community scale' undertakings to establish works councils?

2   Taking a management perspective make a list of the major advantages and disadvantages of the new directive for your organisation (or one with which you are familiar).

Feedback

1   *Why do you think successive UK governments are so cautious about agreeing to measures of the kind found in this Directive and in the earlier one requiring 'community scale' undertakings to establish works councils?*

This is a matter of opinion rather than a matter of fact. Some of the points that could be made are as follows:

- A belief that it imposes additional costs on business, thus reducing its competitiveness, and discouraging job creation.

- A belief that council-type arrangements reduce the level of trust between management and employees, encouraging adversarial employee relations.

- The view that this is not 'the UK way of doing things' and that it would jar with established employee relations systems.

- A general desire to reduce to a minimum the amount of law originating in the EU (i.e. the doctrine of subsidiarity, etc.).

- As a result of the influence exercised on government by larger corporations.

2   *Taking a management perspective make a list of the major advantages and disadvantages of the new directive for your organisation (or one with which you are familiar).*

Answers here will depend on the existing employee relations climate and traditions in the organisation concerned. For those in the habit of consulting and involving employees collectively or individually little will change. More regular 'general' consultative forums will have to be held and be seen to be taken seriously. Otherwise little will change culturally.

By contrast, where there is little existing consultation the new directive, assuming it is effectively policed, will lead to substantial changes. Aside from greater openness, and more questioning of management decisions, there will be significant practical issues to deal with – especially in non-union firms. When and where will meetings be held? Who draws up the agenda and terms of reference? Who organises elections? And so on.

CHAPTER 31 HEALTH, SAFETY AND WELFARE

This is a straightforward, stand-alone chapter looking at all the major issues involved in the management of health, safety and welfare at work. There are three main sections. The first surveys the legal situation as it has evolved in recent years. The key Acts of Parliament and European Directives are outlined, as is the operation of the civil and criminal branches of the law on health and safety. We go on to look first at the management of stress and emotional welfare (a topic which has recently received a great deal of attention in the literature), and second at physical welfare. In this latter section the issue of health and safety training is covered, the area in which HR departments are most involved. Finally we look at the role played by occupational health departments, where they exist.

Additional teaching material

The following article by Helene Ashe-Roy was published as part of a *Financial Times* survey into health and safety matters in 1999. The full report, comprising several very interesting articles, can be read on the FT.com website at 'specials.ft.com/In/health'. In this article the view is put that we are in the process of witnessing a fundamental shift in the context of health and safety at work. It is further argued that this requires new thinking on the part of employers, employees, trade unions and government. The article provides useful supplementary reading to the material found in Chapter 31, looking as it does to the future. Discussion questions and lecturer feedback are provided at the end of the article.

A plea for flexibility

More small businesses, more women in the workforce and a switch from manufacturing to services are presenting completely new challenges.

By Helene Ashe-Roy, *Financial Times*

When the Health and Safety at Work Act was introduced in 1974, around 90 per cent of the workforce worked for large public and private undertakings. The bulk of employment was in the manufacturing industries, union membership was widespread, women made up a minority of the workforce, information technology was a blip on the horizon and preventing accidents, injury and death the main focus of the safety professional.

A quarter of a century on and the parameters of this working world have shifted almost beyond recognition. Manufacturing industries have yielded to service industries, state-owned enterprises have been privatised and fragmented, there has been an explosion of medium, small and micro-sized companies and of the self-employed, union membership has fallen away, around half the workforce is female, large corporations contract out their non-core business, there is a computer in every office – and to the concerns of workplace safety has been added the far less manageable problem of occupational ill health.

Getting on for half the country's workforce is now employed in an estimated 3.5m–5m small companies, and it is here that the ageing Health and Safety at Work Act is at its least effective. Research by the HSE indicates that employees in such undertakings are far more likely to suffer

141

serious injury or death than those in larger concerns. Jacqueline Jeynes, health and safety policy adviser for the Federation of Small Businesses is quick, however, to leap to their defence.

'There is a very small proportion of businesses that is not operating properly and there is nothing we can do about them,' she says. 'Even the Inland Revenue do not know about them. But we resent being tarred with the same brush. And the large organisations are outsourcing their most hazardous operations to improve their insurance premiums, which skews the statistics.

'Small businesses have a much more fluid management style and need a more holistic, flexible approach to enforcement. People from a big business background with formal structures behind them are not always aware of the practical implications for small businesses when putting the European Directives into place at a national level.'

Ms Jeynes is particularly frustrated that there are no representatives from small business organisations on the Health and Safety Commission (HSC), so that their voice is not heard early enough in the planning of health and safety strategy. She is also concerned at the way the government is increasingly shifting responsibilities for social issues on to the employer.

'More and more social issues are being introduced under the banner of health and safety and there is a limit to how much the small employer can take,' she says. 'But the risk assessment approach, once employers have got the hang of it, does offer the sort of flexibility that is fine for small businesses. What they need is sector-specific advice, enough to comply within the context within which they operate, not information overload.'

Graeme Pykett, senior health and safety policy adviser for the CBI, echoes Jacqueline Jeynes' call for more flexibility in health and safety policy. 'The strength of the risk-based approach taken in the UK is that it can adapt to new situations,' he says. 'Regulations need to take into account the needs and abilities of small firms as well as big ones if we want health and safety regulation to support rather than undermine competitiveness. Small firms need clear accessible guidance that sets out what they need to do to manage health and safety risks. They tend to have more informal arrangements and this needs to be recognised and addressed in regulations and guidance.

'The challenge for part-time, contracted and home-based workers is to make sure they are part of the health and safety culture of the company. Management control is more complex but the key is effective communication in both directions, together with training, which takes into account the working environment. Employees also need to be aware that they have responsibilities to act on the advice and instructions given by the employer.'

Small businesses in general are non-unionised. Not surprisingly, the TUC sees greater unionisation as having a direct pay-off in improved health and safety and, at its recent conference, announced a membership recruitment drive as one of its main strategies for the 21st century.

'The growth in small workplaces since 1974 means that inspectors can only visit a fraction of them, so we have to rely on people getting it right without them,' says Owen Tudor, senior health and safety policy adviser at the TUC. 'The safety reps are now more important than ever and they need to be available to workers in more than just the traditional, large workforces. So roving safety representatives, piloted in Sweden, could be used to spread grass roots involvement of worker safety reps to workplaces without internal safety structures.'

The TUC is also concerning itself with the particular health and safety problems of women workers and is calling for the HSE to develop a strategic agenda that is gender-sensitive and reflects the different experiences that half the workforce faces, in particular the growing problems of musculoskeletal disorders and violence at work.

Call centres

'The labour market has seen a growth in the jobs which women do, such as caring, clerical and service jobs,' says Owen Tudor. 'These jobs have traditionally been seen as low risk because our society understates the problems of long-term pain. The balance of injury and ill health has changed from acute to chronic disease and injury.'

If there is one employment sector that typifies the changing nature of the workplace, it is the call centre, which employs many of the new army of women workers and illustrates the shift from acute injury and death to chronic disease, both mental and physical.

Call centres now employ more people in the UK than coal, steel and vehicle production combined. The monotonous and tightly regulated tasks and resulting loss of worker autonomy is leading to growing reports of repetitive strain injuries, hearing damage, stress-related illness and coronary heart disease.

Indecent Exposure, a recent survey by the RNID and the TUC, reports that 39 per cent of call centre workers say that their hearing is being damaged by exposure to noise at work and that their employers are doing little or nothing about it. The existing guidelines to the 1989 Noise at Work Regulations are difficult to apply to non-ambient noise and the report calls for these guidelines to be updated.

One clear indicator of the shift of concern from safety to health-related issues in the modern workplace is the programme of research commissioned by the British Occupational Health Research Foundation. Research topics are chosen by a scientific committee that not only includes representatives from medical and academic institutions but also from the foundation's sponsors among large organisations in both the public and private sectors.

Top of the list come musculo-skeletal disorders, both in the upper limbs and the lower back, closely followed by the management of change, prevention of stress and prevention and treatment of post-traumatic stress disorder. So serious has the problem of stress and mental ill health become in the streamlined, downsized late 20th century workplace that there is a growing call for the HSE to introduce specific legislation to manage it – a call strongly supported by the TUC and equally strongly opposed by the CBI.

But up there among the top five demands for more research is the growing problem of occupational asthma, reflecting partly the ever-multiplying variety of chemicals and other sensitizers used in modern processes and partly the impingement on workplace health of the growing problem of general environmental pollution.

Occupational asthma points a finger at the one certain issue that will have to be faced by health, safety and environment policy makers in the next century, and that is the increased blurring of the boundaries between areas of responsibility; between occupational and public health; between working and private life; between physical and mental illness; between safety within the factory gate and the environment outside it.

'Joined up Thinking'

'It's no longer a matter of protecting our workforce by shoving our nasties up a chimney. It's also about where it goes afterwards,' points out David Bloor of the British Occupational Hygiene Society, succinctly.

Just as the way people work has become more fluid, with multiskilling, job-sharing and hot-desking, so the comfortable compartments between health, safety and environment are breaking down and problems can no longer be viewed in isolation. Joined-up thinking is not just an over-worked government catchphrase, it is also the only way forward 25 years after Robens.

Copyright © The Financial Times Limited 1999. Reproduced with permission.

Questions for discussion

1   Why do you think we are witnessing so little reduction in workplace-related ill-health despite our increasing tendency to work in clean, office-based environments?

2   Use the legal material presented in Chapter 31 to consider what, if any, new legislative measures are going to be needed to tackle the issues set out in the article.

Feedback

1   *Why do you think we are witnessing so little reduction in workplace-related ill-health despite our increasing tendency to work in clean, office-based environments?*

Probable responses are as follows:

- There are physical hazards in many service industry premises, just as in manufacturing environments (e.g. kitchens, storerooms, forms of transport, hospitals, etc.).

- Working environments may be less dangerous, but work is more pressured now and hours worked are longer – leading to stress, burnout, heart attacks, bad diet, etc.

- Many of us spend a great deal of time commuting to work – this makes us tired and more susceptible to illness.

- Job insecurity leading to sleepless nights, presenteeism, etc.

2   *Use the legal material presented in Chapter 31 to consider what, if any, new legislative measures are going to be needed to tackle the issues set out in the article.*

The framework of the law (inspectorate, risk assessments, compensation, etc.) is appropriate for the new environment. What is needed is a shift in HSE and HSC rhetoric and advice, more vocal opinion from trade unions and other bodies, more health and safety inspectors. Health, safety and welfare is inadequately policed at present, with resources being directed at the high-risk environments rather than at more 'typical' workplaces.

CHAPTER 32 GRIEVANCE AND DISCIPLINE

In this chapter we review in some detail topics which are central to the conduct of a professional human resource function, but which are given insufficient attention in the literature. Both grievance and discipline are examined under the general framework of 'organisational justice'. We look at different approaches to the management of these issues, suggesting good practice, and outlining the key features of effective procedures. The central issue of equity is particularly highlighted.

Additional teaching material

The material of this chapter is well suited to conventional lecture treatment. The opening section about the Milgram experiments invariably fascinates students and provides an excellent basis for considering why people comply with authority and the problems of non-compliance. The following sections considering the nature of grievance and discipline and the framework of organisational justice are also suitable, using Figures 32.1, 32.2, 32.3 and 32.4 as organising features.

Other possibilities are:

(a)   Discuss the material in the Window on Practice about petty pilfering at work. Which of those actions would members of the group regard as reasonable, and why?

(b)   Small group discussion on the question posed at the close of the chapter, 'Are grievance and discipline processes equitable?'

(c)   Discuss Activity 32.3.

(d)   A quick exercise that will leave them talking! After an introduction emphasising the importance of speed and accuracy, pass out the questionnaire to the students, making sure that they place it face down in front of them. Then count down, 'Five … four … three … two … one … start NOW.'

Questionnaire

Read through to the end of the questionnaire carefully before answering any of the questions.

1   What is the next number in this sequence?

        17   35   44   64   85 …

2   Write down your mother's first name …

3   Multiply 6 by 13 and shout out the answer

4   What is the title of the person who chairs proceedings in the House of Commons? …

5   What is the price of a first class postage stamp? …

6   Tear a strip of approximately one inch width off the top of this questionnaire and hide it.

7   Ten men and three women enter a lift on the ground floor. It rises to floor 7, where two men and one woman get out and three children get in. It then rises to floor 12, where all the children get out and the remaining two women. It rises to floor 15 where six men get out and four women get in. It then rises to floor 20, where everyone gets out, while seven men and eight women get in. The lift goes down to floor 14, where all but two women get out. They are then joined by four men, six women and three children for the descent to the ground floor. How many men ... women ..., and children ... have travelled for more than ten floors in either direction?

8   If your birthday is between January and June, take off your left shoe and put it on the desk in front of you. If your birthday is between July and December, take off your right shoe and put it on the floor behind your chair.

9   What is the capital city of Peru? ...

10   Having read through to the end, as instructed at the head of the page, answer question 1 only.

Unless they have been caught out before, you can be sure that the majority of the group will **not** read through to the end first, but will start answering the questions.

Topics for subsequent discussion are:

- Why did so many people disobey the clear instruction at the head of the page? (Conflict of instructions mean that they respond to the *person* of the lecturer rather than to the written word ... emphasis on speed makes that an imperative which overrides the need for accuracy and care ... the fact that it is a competitive exercise distorts normal judgement.)

- To what extent do people hear or read what they expect rather than what is transmitted to them? (Refer back to Chapter 7 on communication.)

- Are there any examples of this behaviour from working life?

- How do you get over these problems?

Reading assignment

Read Milgram (1974) and consider to what extent the results would have been different if the subjects had been either (a) women or (b) of a different nationality.

Individual assignment

Consider the situation in any organisation to decide whether or not the elements of the organisational justice framework are present. What (if any) are missing and how could they be provided?

Case study

Here is a short case study illustrating the some of the practical problems associated with the management of disciplinary issues at work. The case concerns a teacher perceived to be incapable of carrying out his job to the expected standard. Discussion questions and tutor feedback are provided at the end.

The failing teacher

In 1997 there was concern within the Department for Education and Employment that a small minority of school teachers lacked sufficient capability to discharge their duties satisfactorily. The minister of education at the time, Stephen Byers, required all local authorities and boards of governors to introduce capability procedures to ensure that such teachers were either helped to improve their performance or removed from teaching.

This was an unusual initiative in comparison with other fields of employment, as there were already procedures to deal with misconduct and ill-health. Adding a separate procedure to deal with capability was a novelty; most organisations have a single procedure to deal with the broad concept of discipline, as described in the chapter, which would include capability. It is also unusual for issues of capability to be handled through procedural machinery.

In 2001 Mr B was Head of The High School, with just over 1,000 pupils. He described teacher capability this way:

> 'There are certain basic qualities and skills that a teacher needs. If they lack
> more than one, they are incapable. The required skills and qualities are:

- To control children collectively and individually.

- To motivate them by providing lessons which are interesting and from which children learn.

- Sound subject knowledge.

- Open-mindedness to adapt and take on new skills.

Mr B had a problem with a Maths teacher, Mr N, who was not strong on class organisation and children often took advantage of him. An official inspection identified weaknesses in planning, teaching and use of resources. With a lot of support and assistance from colleagues there was improvement, but five years later the next official inspection involved inspectors observing classes and these were found to be unsatisfactory, with a test that was poorly planned and poorly organised. There was weak supervision, with the teacher telling the pupils to shut up. The inspection report criticised the Head of Maths for lack of monitoring and taking action, and criticised the teacher for refusing to follow guidelines. Mr B reported the matter to the governors who decided to employ a consultant to work with Mr N. The consultant confirmed what the inspectors had said and made suggestions, which Mr N did not follow, by now being in a frame of mind where everyone else was wrong.

Mr B saw Mr N and said that capability procedures would now be started. The following day Mr N sent in a sick note from his GP saying he was suffering from exhaustion. He never returned to the school. After intervention by the LEA Personnel Department, Mr N was persuaded to resign with six months' pay in lieu of notice.

Questions for discussion

1   How would you assess the effectiveness of the way this matter was handled?

2   As Mr N was demonstrably ineffective over some years, why was he not dismissed?

3   How would you have improved on Mr B's handling of the matter?

Feedback

1   *How would you assess the effectiveness of the way this matter was handled?*

There was diffidence by Mr N's seniors in keeping a close eye on the problem. The Head of Department claimed it was not his job to act as a nursemaid. Other colleagues felt that they had 'done their bit' by providing some initial support. The Head, Mr B, had wanted to believe that all was well.

For unsatisfactory teaching to continue for five years is inexcusable. The decision of the governors to employ a consultant was further prevarication and merely prolonged the agony for everyone. A colleague said:

> 'The Maths Dept was demoralised by the situation. The Head of Department doubts anybody's judgement about others' teaching and has appalling management. When he was appointed Mr N was the only candidate and could have walked in to any one of six other jobs, but he was more trouble than he was worth and the whole process ruined his life.'

2   *As Mr N was demonstrably ineffective over some years, why was he not dismissed?*

The convention within teaching has always been that one is only dismissed for ill-health or misconduct. Dismissal on the grounds of lacking capability (in the way described by Mr B) is difficult to demonstrate to a tribunal and LEAs are extremely anxious to avoid the costs of tribunal hearings. Cases of alleged unfair dismissal on these grounds are rare at tribunals.

3   *How would you have improved on Mr B's handling of the matter?*

The value of this question is to see what understanding there is of the difficulty in this type of situation. The members of the group who answer along the lines that it is appalling, and 'would never happen where I work', are probably wrong. Although terminations in the early stages of employment are relatively common, the handling of problems of capability where the employee has over seven years' service is frequently fudged.

The more obvious answers are:

(a)   Sustained close supervision and guidance from senior colleagues to develop the self-discipline in Mr N that is clearly missing, with reference back to opening of chapter.

(b)   Some team teaching so that Mr N has the benefit of example and support from his colleagues.

(c)   Much more prompt and more decisive action by the Head and the governors.

(d)   Avoid using procedure to deal with this type of capability issue.

It would be worth reminding students of the managerial dilemma in any organisation dismissing staff who have scarce skills. Head teachers and LEAs tend to be cautious about getting at cross-purposes with trade unions. Despite this Mr N got his settlement without union representation: he had not paid his subscription!

CHAPTER 33 INTERACTIVE SKILL: GRIEVANCE AND DISCIPLINARY INTERVIEWING

In this chapter the focus shifts from the theoretical issues surrounding grievance and disciplinary processes to the practicalities. We look in turn at effective ways of carrying out grievance and then disciplinary interviews, from preparation through execution to disengagement.

Additional teaching material

We suggest that a practical session based on the material in Chapter 33 should start by getting agreement to the proposition that grievance and disciplinary processes are problem solving. That is why discussion of discipline is kept separate here from discussion of dismissal. Unfortunately some managers think of discipline as only a preparation for dismissal. The following is a suggested plan. Briefing for the three exercises referred to follows.

1 Open with a short talk reiterating the opening argument of the chapter. Test acceptance of the argument with one or two questions.

2 Ask if there are any suggestions in answer to the question in Activity 33.1. Encourage students to think of examples at school or in sporting situations if they do not have work experience.

3 Explain the nature of grievance and disciplinary interviewing.

4 Try running Exercise 33.1 in pairs, with one person describing an incident and the other reflecting back a summary to get confirmation of correct understanding.

5 Move on to Exercise 33.2, but introduce it with care, as you want the people to 'talk real stuff', but they will be very inhibited. You probably have to work with volunteers only, allowing others to go to the library. Also, make it clear that there is no concluding discussion. All that will happen is that two people will talk to each other in the way described.

6 Have a general group discussion about the professional weeper and the counter-attacker.

7 Tina Tietjen's book, *I'd like to Have a Word With You* (1987), was written to accompany a video presentation on disciplinary interviewing produced by Video Arts. It may be useful to show the video.

Three practical exercises

Here are three practical exercises for you to try. Each should stimulate thinking about different aspects of handling grievance and disciplinary matters in the workplace.

Exercise 33.1

Reflection is a specialised technique, which is especially appropriate for grievance and discipline. It is reflecting back something a respondent has said in order to get more comment on the same topic. It has been defined by W.E. Beveridge as:

> a selective form of listening in which the listener picks out the emotional overtones of a statement and 'reflects' these back to the respondent without any attempt to evaluate them . . . the interviewer expresses neither approval or disapproval, neither sympathy or condemnation. (1968, p. 57)

In the next few conversations you have, practise reflection and see what effect it has on the development of the exchanges with the other person. Then think further about the type of discipline and grievance situations in which reflection would be useful.

Exercise 33.2

This exercise needs the co-operation of your spouse, other trusted relative or close friend.

1   Identify an incident that the other person experienced some time in the past, which was unpleasant or disconcerting at the time, and about which your friend feels either guilty or that they were unfairly treated.

2   Take the respondent through the events again, using the methods suggested in this chapter, including decision making to agree on what should have been done.

3   Change roles and repeat the process with an incident from your past.

Exercise 33.3

In the booklet *I'd Like to Have a Word With You*, Tina Tietjen identifies ten categories of difficult respondent in disciplinary interviews. One of these is 'the professional weeper':

> This is the person who can turn on tears like turning on a tap. Some people are quite unmoved by tears, but lots of bosses find tears and emotion very hard to cope with. They are either very embarrassed or very apologetic that their words could have had such an effect. (Tietjen 1987, p. 26)

How would you respond to the professional weeper? Can you recall a situation when you have had to cope with tears and emotion? How will you do it next time?

Another of her categories is 'the counter-attacker' who

> operates on the maxim that the best defence is attack. Once you have stated your reasons for the interview, he will leap straight into the discussion, relishing the opportunity to 'have it out'. The obvious danger is that you will respond to his aggression, that a battle of words will ensue and nothing else will happen.

How would you respond to the counter-attacker? Do you find it difficult to avoid rising to the bait of being drawn into an argument? How will you do it next time?

Now get your close friend to play one of these roles of professional weeper or counter-attacker, while you play the part of the manager.

PART 6 CASE STUDY FEEDBACK

Inevitably the strike was resolved by discussion between the two parties and a modification to the management position. The initial management position of apparent intractability was one genuinely believed to be unalterable due to the airline's competitive position in the marketplace. There was also a significant degree of asserting managerial prerogative and calling the union's bluff. The strike itself was very damaging to business volume, management credibility, passenger reaction and shareholder approval. The bottom-line effect was substantial. An official estimate by British Airways that their profitability for that year declined by £124 million due to the strike. The eventual settlement apparently will eventually achieve the financial savings that were needed, following consultation with union officials.

The following particular points are worth noting:

1   Two unions representing the same group of employees is a major problem, unless there are good collaborative arrangements between them. In this case the unions were competing with each other. Management had perhaps encouraged only one, but the situation remained dangerous. An incident of this type seemed inevitable. Whoever or whatever was to blame, it remained a *management* problem that had not been resolved.

2   This was a 'middle class' strike, by people who largely found such actions repugnant and humiliating. Despite their reluctance, they were prepared to take the action, demonstrating considerable alienation.

3   The majority tactic of reporting sick rather than taking strike action perhaps indicated a high degree of apprehension about the possibility of management 'reprisals', or a more calculated attitude of avoiding pay deductions. It was highly disruptive, as some people were given medical notes by their GPs to cover a much longer period than the action lasted. Furthermore there was a concerted, angry reaction by local GPs, objecting to their practices being hijacked by industrial action.

CHAPTER 34 STRATEGIC ASPECTS OF PAYMENT

In this chapter we introduce the subject of pay management by looking at the major strategic choices that employers face when determining two key questions:

- how much people should be paid;

- in what form the pay package should be made up.

These are explored in two sections, one focusing on alternative methods for establishing rates of pay, another describing the main elements that can be included in a pay packet. Prior to this we set the scene for these decisions by assessing what are the employer's and employee's objectives for 'the contract of payment'. Towards the end of the chapter we reflect on the importance of equity in pay policy and on the academic debate about the extent to which pay management in the UK has become more 'strategic' in recent years.

Additional teaching material

Exercise 34.1

The following article by Lucy Kellaway is light-hearted and witty, but it also raises several interesting questions about relative pay levels. It is a good basis for a wide-ranging discussion about organisational policy in respect of pay. Discussion questions and lecturer feedback are provided at the end of the article.

Pandora's pay packet

By Lucy Kellaway, FT.com site, 14 May 2001

PLEASE DON'T TELL ME WHAT YOU'RE PAID, I COULDN'T COPE WITH THE STRESS.

Imagine if you got into work to find you had been sent an e-mail listing the salaries and bonuses of everybody in your company.

You'd fall on it, read it greedily. And then read it again. You'd scan the list for all those paid more than you. All those paid less. You'd look up the salaries of your most comparable colleagues. You'd look for those of the cocky ones whom you've never rated.

Assuming that you had started the day feeling reasonably content with your salary, by the end it would be a different story. Either you'd be seething at the higher salaries paid to people you think less deserving than yourself, or you'd be feeling sheepish about those talented hardworking people earning considerably less than you.

This is what happens in a case study in the latest *Harvard Business Review*. A disaffected employee unearths a complete salary and bonus list and promptly e-mails it to the entire staff. Sure enough, all hell breaks loose.

The four labour market experts wheeled on by the magazine to discuss the case agree on one thing. The forced disclosure will do some good – it will bring about a more open culture and a fairer pay system.

I think this is optimistic. Openness is not a good thing *per se*. It is good only when the occasion calls for it.

Pay is the last taboo. Pay is full of iniquities and will always be so. Better, therefore, not to draw attention to it.

If you meet someone at a dinner party, you can ask them about their religion. You can ask them which way they are going to vote. You can ask what they paid for their house. (In fact, I consider this to be the height of bad manners but people ask, nevertheless.)

You may even, if circumstances are right, be able to ask about their sex lives. What you cannot do, under any circumstances, is ask how much they are paid.

You could say that this reticence is misplaced and that in time pay will go the way of all the other taboos.

The reason salaries are so sensitive is that they are the only 'objective' way we have of comparing your labour to mine. Your salary is a clear measure of what someone else is prepared to pay for you.

This makes pay more revealing than other kinds of financial information.

If I know you paid a lot for your house I can conclude any number of things. That your salary is huge. Or that your wife's is. That one or other of you inherited some money. Or that you made a couple of lucky property moves in the past. There are all kinds of possibilities.

But your salary measures only one thing: it sums up your worth. Only as we all know, it does nothing of the kind.

While it may be dangerous to discuss salaries at a dinner party, where bankers may be cheek by jowl with teachers, to discuss them in the office canteen is dynamite.

If salaries in your company were determined fairly, according to some commonly agreed principle, secrecy might not be necessary. But they aren't determined like that, are they? In the real world, your salary reflects a thousand different things, your 'worth' being only one of them.

When did you join the company? Was the job market tight at the time? Which department are you in? How well does your boss like you? How good are you at complaining? All these things affect your pay.

In the public sector people traditionally knew what others were paid, because for each grade and each task there was a rate. But now, thanks to performance-related pay, salary discussion is becoming taboo there too.

Some trendy new companies have experimented with full salary disclosure. This tends to work when the company is very young but as it grows and the outside labour market bears down, transparency seems like less of a good thing.

It could be argued that by publishing all salaries in a company you shock the system into greater 'fairness'. But even if this did happen, it is doubtful whether it would be desirable. Would you want to own shares in a company that could not hire good people from the outside at higher wages for fear of alienating existing employees?

We have, under our noses, a good example of what happens when individual salaries are forcibly outed. For the past few years, directors of public companies have had to disclose in full, gory detail how much they are paid. The aim of this was to rein in the worst of the fat cat pay increases.

Yet it is debatable whether it has in fact achieved that. Pay levels of top directors have continued to soar and the supposed performance criteria they have held up to justify their bonuses have proved to be laughably easy to meet. Maybe they would have risen still further if disclosure had not been required; maybe they would not.

What transparency at the top has certainly done is to make everyone else's sense of outrage and envy all the greater. Now that the fat cat is out of the bag, we can all see how fat it really is – and the sight does us no good at all.

So I am not going to tell you what I earn, either. More than anything else, I do not want to share this information with my colleagues.

Yet suppose when I get into work tomorrow I find that e-mail waiting for me. Will I heed the above and simply press the 'delete' button? Like hell. I'll fall on it, read it greedily, then read it again.

Contact Lucy Kellaway.

Copyright © The Financial Times 2001. Reproduced with permission.

Questions for discussion

1   Is pay really 'the last taboo' as is argued in this article?

2   Why is it only 'dangerous' to discuss salaries at a dinner party, but 'dynamite' to discuss them in the office canteen?

3   Is the author right to argue that more openness in the area of pay is not something to be welcomed?

Feedback

1   *Is pay really 'the last taboo' as is argued in this article?*

Views will differ on this question. It is true that people are often reluctant for others to know what they are paid and will seek to keep the information under wraps, but this is very much a middle class/professional/managerial concern. It is in these fields that people perceive 'their worth' to be signalled in some form by their salary, and in which they fear the reaction of others if it is disclosed. Someone earning £40,000 a year, for example, may think that they will be perceived poorly by someone else earning £70,000 or that they will be regarded as grossly overpaid by someone earning £15,000 a year. In either case it is better to keep the figure a secret.

For the majority of people working in other occupations and in the public sector, pay is not such a taboo. Here hourly rates and annual salaries are well known and so no attempt is made to conceal them. Pay rates are an issue of conversation, but they are anything but a taboo.

2   *Why is it only 'dangerous' to discuss salaries at a dinner party, but 'dynamite' to discuss them in the office canteen?*

The issue here is perceived equity and the distinction between differentials and relativities discussed in Chapter 34. There is an expectation that pay rates will vary substantially from one employer to another, even within the same profession. Individuals who are relatively poorly paid may not like this, but they know:

(a)   that they can try to move to another employment if they wish to; and

(b)   that some employers can afford to pay more than others.

In other words, it is an accepted fact of working life. This is not the case within an organisation, where people expect to be treated fairly *vis-à-vis* one another. Hence, discovering that a colleague is paid much more than you for doing a similar job, or one that is perceived to be of equal or lower status, is 'dynamite'. It can be seriously upsetting and can induce substantial feelings of anger. Major inequity in pay is a big demotivator and a destabiliser of working relationships. Organisations can thus choose between having a 'feels-fair' system which is open or an inequitable one which is kept confidential. It is the potential consequences of this choice which the Kellaway article explores.

3   *Is the author right to argue that more openness in the area of pay is not something to be welcomed?*

Lucy Kellaway is effectively arguing for the second of these options. She is saying that it is preferable for both employers and employees to run a confidential pay system which may not be entirely equitable, than an open one which is.

The argument for this position is based on the notion that pay never will be seen as 'equitable' however it is determined, because people always rate their own worth rather more highly than their organisations do. In open systems, pay will thus always be something of a 'running sore' and is best not disclosed.

It can also be argued that running an equitable pay system (e.g. one based on an analytical job evaluation system) can hold organisations back. It makes it harder for them to compete in tight labour markets by rewarding individuals and groups who are hard to attract. It is better to let the market determine salaries, accept that this leads to unfairness, but try to make sure people don't know about it.

The argument against this is that it is not possible to keep pay rates secret. Information of this kind leaks out and spreads. Sometimes exaggerated rumours about what people are paid get around. For this reason it is best to take the first option and go for a fair and open system. You can still pay market supplements to secure the services of hard-to-recruit people, but you do so openly and only when the decision can clearly be justified objectively.

Exercise 34.2

A suggested topic for a classroom debate:

Money is the only significant motivator of working performance

Pro

Very few people indeed would undertake employment if they were not paid more for working than for not working. Not only does income from employment provide the opportunity for increasing one's material possessions, it is also the main indicator of status and personal achievement. The importance of money as a motivator has been underplayed by academic researchers simply because it closes an otherwise fruitful line of enquiry. Once the significance of money is established, then there is no interest in research about participation, job design, improving communication, quality of working life and all the never-ending variations that research has proposed. Managers are also susceptible to this line of argument as it justifies their existence and makes their job sound more difficult, so they can describe themselves as leaders and convince their friends that they have some rare ability to 'handle people'. When told of an opportunity to earn more money most people are drawn by that feature much more than by other aspects, like the nature of the new job. Businesses *always* increase the pay rates of people as they move up the hierarchy, even though there could be an argument to say that money loses its importance because of other motivators, like status and perquisites. When offered early retirement, the majority of people accept, if the money is right.

Con

Money is important as an indication of something else. The high salary is valued by its recipient mainly as a measure of worth and achievement. Those are the motivators: not the money. Also the money becomes important as that type of indicator only when other indicators are absent. Those with intrinsically satisfying jobs or with some other indication of social esteem are less concerned about their income than those whose jobs are boring or who feel disparaged by their fellows. One of the principles of incentive pay schemes is that there should be a clear linkage between payment and the performance that produces it, yet most pay increases are divorced from individual performance and linked to changes in the cost of living or skill scarcity. When pay does not discriminate between recipients it can not motivate.

CHAPTER 35 JOB EVALUATION

This chapter follows on from the sections of Chapter 34 that are concerned with establishing the level of pay. Here the focus is on internal differentials (i.e. the rate of pay associated with each job in an organisation). We start by describing traditional forms of grading structure and discuss the current trend towards 'broadbanding' in which the number of separate grades is reduced to allow greater flexibility. We go on to discuss the implementation of job evaluation, looking at different systems and criteria for establishing the worth of one job *vis-à-vis* that of another. The final section focuses in some detail on the role that the expectations of equal pay law *should* (not *do*) play in determining pay rates.

Additional teaching material

This article, dating from May 2001, reports the government's future intentions in the field of equal pay – a topic dealt with towards the end of Chapter 35. A few weeks after this article was written (with the General Election safely behind it) the government announced that it was not going to give women returning from maternity leave any *right* to work on a part-time basis. Discussion questions and lecturer feedback are provided at the end of the article.

Employment minister fires the latest shots in equal pay battle

By Rosemary Bennett, FT.com website, 8 May 2001

Sweeping changes to equal pay employment tribunals will be unveiled on Tuesday by Tessa Jowell, employment minister.

She is expected to announce amendments to the 30-year-old Equal Pay Act to speed up tribunals by replacing the existing system of rival reports from different experts with a single independent assessor for each case.

Under the plans, groups of employees bringing cases will be able to make one joint application with one set of paperwork.

Ms Jowell calls tribunals, which can currently take up to four years to reach a conclusion, 'a last resort' for dealing with the 'totally unacceptable' 18 per cent pay gap between men and women.

Changing the law is the easy bit, she said in an interview. 'Using the law to simplify and speed up the tribunal process is obviously a necessary step, but it is easier than tackling the underlying cause of the pay discrimination, a far more complex area,' she said.

However, Ms Jowell believes the legal changes, along with the minimum wage and other economic factors, will combine over the next decade to narrow the pay gap more dramatically than at any time since the Act was passed.

She is undaunted by the scale of the problem.

Women are clustered even now in the 10 lowest paid groups and are particularly penalised if they go part-time. Then there is the problem of employers simply paying female staff less for the same work done by their male counterparts.

Ms Jowell recently appointed Denise Kingsmill, deputy chairman of the Competition Commission, to head a Women's Employment and Pay Review, to promote the benefits of equal pay to employers who have enjoyed the lower wage bills that come with pay discrimination.

Ms Kingsmill has said she will use pay-as-you-earn data to name sectors that systematically pay women less than men.

Government departments will be audited next year to ensure that Whitehall's own house is in order before ministers start criticising others. For those private sector companies that volunteer to audit their wage bills for discrimination, there will be Castle Awards, named after Barbara Castle, the Labour minister who presided over the original Equal Pay Act.

'I hope in the future when women go for interview they will routinely ask whether the prospective employer has a Castle Award,' Ms Jowell says.

But is exhortation enough to make companies add to their costs with pay rises for women?

'If companies fail to address this issue women will not want to work for them and those businesses will be left fishing in half the pool when it comes to recruiting,' she said.

The Confederation of British Industry has backed the review – a coup for Ms Jowell. But the CBI has made its opposition plain to another government initiative related to the drive for equal pay – the work/life balance. Ministers are wrestling with this seemingly intractable problem and, in particular, whether mothers returning from maternity leave should have the right to work part-time.

Rigid working practices in many businesses contribute to the low productivity and pay of female returners who often 'downshift' into a job with more flexibility than one making full use of their skills and qualifications.

The government looks set to establish an independent commission to make recommendations on the issue.

Ms Jowell declines to comment on the final decision, but has been researching which employers are making the most of female staff.

Unilever, the food and consumer products group, boasts a 90% record on women returning from maternity leave, saving significant recruitment costs, largely due to the flexible package it offers, she claims. Women can take career breaks of up to five years, on condition that they work a month a year, at home if they wish, in order to keep up-to-date on skills and in touch with working life.

That is something Ms Jowell would like the government to emulate. She sees the New Deal for lone parents and partners as a way of keeping mothers in touch with the world of work even if they do not intend rejoining the workforce for several years. 'These are the crucial candidates to help first, but I hope in time the working age agency will be able to offer the same support to all women'.

Copyright © The Financial Times Group 2001. Reproduced with permission.

Questions for discussion

1   Make a list of the different initiatives mentioned in the article which have as one of their purposes equalising pay rates between men and women.

2   To what extent do you think these initiatives will have the desired effect?

3   Is job evaluation the best way of establishing how much men and women in the same organisation should be paid?

4   What other forms of government intervention might make a contribution to the achievement of equal pay?

Feedback

1   *Make a list of the different initiatives mentioned in the article which have as one of their purposes equalising pay rates between men and women.*

(a)   Modifications to employment tribunal procedure.

(b)   National minimum wage.

(c)   'Naming and shaming' of sectors with a poor equal pay record.

(d)   Government setting an example.

(e)   A kitemark-type awards system.

(f)   Strengthened rights for women with children.

(g)   New deal initiatives.

2   *To what extent do you think these initiatives will have the desired effect?*

This is clearly a matter of opinion. Ministers argue that these are major public policy initiatives which will combine to improve matters considerably. It is, however, possible to take a more cynical position and to see them as a means for government to appear to be tackling an issue while actually doing very little. The initiatives could be seen as being principally about public relations ahead of an election, when really they are a means of kicking the issue forward into the long grass. Government will shy away from taking any steps that are too radical for fear of alienating its business supporters.

3   *Is job evaluation the best way of establishing how much men and women in the same organisation should be paid?*

The answer here depends on what you understand by the word 'best'. It is the case that job evaluation is the fairest means of measuring the relative worth of different jobs. No better system has been invented. However, this means that it is job focused rather than people focused and that it is not suited to measuring the performance of individual employees in the jobs. For fairness between men and women to be established there thus needs to be a combination of job evaluation *and* some form of performance measurement system which operates without sex bias.

4   *What other forms of government intervention might make a contribution to the achievement of equal pay?*

The main alternative type of system is a legal regime which operates like the one in Ontario described in Chapter 35 on p. 591. Unlike the current UK system, this does not rely on individual aggrieved employees bringing cases. Instead, rather like our health and safety regime (*see* Chapter 31) there is a government inspectorate with a policing role. The main argument against such a system is its cost and also its tendency to impose further bureaucratic requirements on businesses which already believe themselves to be over-regulated and thus less able to compete effectively.

CHAPTER 36 INCENTIVES

In Chapter 36 we focus on different forms of payment system; on the pay packet rather than the rate of pay. After a short discussion about the evidence on how widely incentive schemes are used in the UK, we go on to look in turn at each of the major types of scheme. We start with the most common, payment by results, going on to assess the merits of performance-related pay, skills-based pay and profit-sharing schemes. In each case we identify the main advantages and disadvantages, draw attention to research in these areas and suggest in what circumstances each type of approach has most to offer.

Additional teaching material

The following article is a short opinion piece on the subject of share options and similar incentive schemes. It takes an international perspective but makes a number of points that are particularly relevant to UK firms. Discussion questions and lecturer feedback are provided at the end of the article.

How the rich get richer

By Robert Taylor, *Financial Times,* 6 December 2000

In today's fierce competition for talent, companies like to use democratic language such as 'empowerment' and 'diversity', 'team-working' and 'partnership', to describe the way they organise their employees. But is this simply the continuation of familiar control and command systems in disguise?

The annual report by Towers Perrin, the international consultants, on remuneration packages in 26 countries provides evidence that may help to answer the question. Its main finding is that an increasing number of companies are using share options and other long-term incentives to attract and retain staff at a time of tightening labour markets.

In 1996 only 10 out of the 26 countries surveyed offered such long-term incentive programmes. The number has now risen to 19 and a phenomenon that was once almost entirely confined to the US has been spreading. 'Stock incentives are providing employers with powerful tools to align employee and shareholder interests,' notes Towers Perrin. 'It is strengthening the levels of employee commitment and engagement and retaining key employees in an increasingly competitive business environment.'

The survey indicates, however, that share options and similar financial inducements are confined to the most senior staff. True, these remuneration packages are spreading down from executives in the boardroom to senior and middle management as well as so-called team leaders. But few companies seem prepared to include all their employees. It is no wonder that, in the US and the UK in particular, reward inequalities between the top 10 per cent and the rest are widening dramatically. This seems surprising if, as companies suggest, commercial performance depends on the loyalty and commitment of all employees – not just the lucky few they choose to reward.

As Towers Perrin concludes: 'Time and again we have seen that as employees take on more responsibility for contributing to bottom-line results, they want to share in those results.' But if the emphasis in companies is on creating flatter organisations, devolving power and responsibility to their staff, it seems invidious that the reward packages are not correspondingly divided among everybody. Surely a team leader's success depends on the efforts of all in the team?

In practice, companies can use incentive schemes not only to reward their favourites but also to punish those they dislike or who they believe do not fit into the company culture. It is certainly hard to devise share option and incentive schemes that operate even-handedly, especially if they are awarded under cover of confidentiality. Instead of encouraging greater performance, such schemes can fuel resentment that may damage the company's reputation and employment success.

Towers Perrin is right to warn companies that are promoting incentive packages to a select few on their payroll. It argues: 'Stock ownership programmes are not a panacea for success. They are one type of reward mechanism that must be carefully considered and, if implemented, done so thoughtfully within the context of an organisation's total rewards strategy and overall business.' At least systems of basic pay and benefits are usually constructed on transparent and understandable principles and negotiated in the open.

Interestingly the latest annual salary survey by Monks Partnership for people employed in the financial sector in the City of London reveals a clear shift from discretionary bonus schemes to a 'more mechanistic' type to ensure 'bonus schemes can be seen by management (particularly overseas headquarters) and staff as equitable and made for the achievement of real, recognisable targets'.

The Towers Perrin report shows that UK chief executives and accountants are the highest paid when compared with colleagues of the same rank in all other European countries surveyed. Argentina has the best-paid human resource directors, followed by the US, Brazil, Belgium and the UK. But is anybody really suggesting that the overall measurable real performance of the UK's executives and senior managers surpasses that of their equivalents in Germany and France? You only have to look at the productivity achievements of the UK and its main European competitors (a gap of 20 to 30 per cent between France or Germany and the UK) to know the answer to that question.

Surely the time has come for companies across western market economies to practice what they preach. The spread of share options and other incentives is welcome – but the rewards should be provided in a more systematic, rigorous and fair manner. Cronyism is not a vice confined to political life. It remains an unjustifiable but ubiquitous phenomenon across the corporate world as well.

Towers Perrin, <u>*Worldwide Total Remuneration Report.*</u>

The report is also available in French, Chinese, German, Italian, Japanese, Spanish and Portuguese.

Copyright © The Financial Times Limited 2000. Reproduced with permission.

Questions for discussion

1 Why are governments increasingly inclined to develop tax-advantageous share ownership schemes of the kind discussed in this article?

2 Why are companies more inclined to offer share option and share ownership schemes to the senior staff than to the workforce as a whole?

3 Do you agree with Robert Taylor that there is a good case for extending access to these incentives to the whole workforce in a company?

Feedback

1 *Why are governments increasingly inclined to develop tax-advantageous share ownership schemes of the kind discussed in this article?*

The straightforward answer is because they want to encourage employers to offer the schemes. They like them for a number of reasons:

- The belief that they encourage constructive (rather than adversarial) employee relations, by making employees and unions identify with organisational interests.

- A belief that it is fair for profits to be shared with those who help make them

2 *Why are companies more inclined to offer share option and share ownership schemes to the senior staff than to the workforce as a whole?*

- Doubts over the extent to which there is employee demand (especially for share schemes which carry a considerable risk).

- Administrative complexity of offering them to all.

- The view that they only realistically work as an incentive for senior staff because it is they who, through their decisions and actions, really influence profit levels.

- Because they are an expected part of senior pay packages and are thus necessary as a means of attracting and retaining high-flyers.

3   *Do you agree with Robert Taylor that there is a good case for extending access to these incentives to the whole workforce in a company?*

This depends on your views about the points made above. Demand is the key issue here. Do employees want to own shares in their own organisations? If they do not, then there is little point in setting up a scheme and no long-term incentive effect. It is better to go for other forms of profit sharing such as are described in Chapter 36.

CHAPTER 37 PENSIONS AND BENEFITS

The third central element of pay policy is the focus of this chapter; namely the growing role played by benefits of one kind or another. We give most attention to occupational pensions, because they are the most common and by far the most costly form of employee benefit. Particular attention here is given to the role of pensions in achieving HRM objectives, but we also take readers through the different kinds of scheme and the main merits of each. Later sections deal respectively with sick pay schemes, company cars and London allowances. In each case we include up-to-date facts and figures as well as assessing the advantages and disadvantages of different approaches. We end with a look at the very topical subject of flexible benefits systems. As yet these are not widespread in the UK, but the case for their use is strong, so we can expect to see considerable growth in the near future.

Additional teaching material

The following article by Sathnam Sanghera puts forward an interesting perspective on employee benefits. Far from being in the employee's interest, it is argued, they are a sophisticated means of increasing our working hours. The article also gives some interesting examples of elements beginning to become common in the benefits packages of US employees. The article was published as part of a *Financial Times* Survey on work/life balance issues. The full report is available on the FT.com website. Discussion questions and lecturer feedback are provided at the end of the article.

BENEFITS PACKAGES: Flaws in the perfect work environment

All-embracing company benefits packages may simply be extending time away from home.

By Sathnam Sanghera, *Financial Times,* 2000

There was a time when a company benefits package was a straightforward thing. Companies would offer health insurance, pension plans and, if they were feeling particularly generous, a handful of stock options.

However, with the ever-tightening labour market, there seem to be no bounds to what perks companies are prepared to offer to retain precious employees. In the US, and, increasingly in the UK too, services including gift shopping and dry cleaning delivery are becoming standard.

In an effort to stick out, some US companies now offer hairstyling salons, masseurs and manicurists on-site. CDW Computer Centers, a computer distributor based in Vernon Hills, Illinois, gives staff free bagels and fruit every Tuesday and free ice cream in the summer. Arcnet, a technology company in New Jersey, goes as far as presenting BMW cars to staff with more than a year's service.

Salomon Smith Barney, the investment bank, has even offered free toothbrushes and underwear to its analysts.

Indeed, in their never-ending efforts to create the perfect environment for employees, some companies are turning workplaces into all-embracing worlds, where employees can literally do everything they need – from swimming, shopping and praying, to breast-feeding and even sleeping. (Yarde Metals in Bristol, Connecticut, encourages sleeping at work to keep people alert.)

However, welfare experts are beginning to question whether any of these benefits packages actually improve the lot of the employee. They might increase loyalty and provide a temporary boost in morale, but is there a danger that employees will find themselves working even longer hours, with subsequent risks to health and productivity?

After all, there is no proof that benefits packages are making life any better for Americans and Europeans. Indeed, while benefit packages get larger, there is increasing evidence that people are working a lot harder and longer than ever before. According to a recent Families and Work Institute Study, 16 per cent of US workers bring work home more than once a week, up from 6 per cent in 1977.

Cary Cooper, BUPA professor of organisational psychology and health at UMIST, in the UK, says that many of the companies that provide elaborate perks are overlooking what employees really need – 'flextime' where they can plan their working day – even if they work from home – around their personal schedules, including childcare and looking after older family.

'I don't see how it can be a perk to have a napping room at work. It will just make you work longer and make sure you see your children less and have less leisure time,' says Mr Cooper. 'Also, perks like cleaning services and a company gym are no compensation for a lack of time with your family.

'These perks don't create a good work–life balance. What people need is shorter working hours and flexible working.' There seems to be a real risk that benefits packages will blur the line between work and home life so much that people will eventually be in 'work mode' all the time.

Fortune magazine's third annual survey to determine the 100 Best Companies to Work for in America, published in January, showed that ever-increasing aspects of private life are being subsumed into company existence. Out of the 100 companies, about 46 offered take-home meals and 25 offered personal concierge services – up from 15 two years ago.

No part of an employee's life, however intimate, is now beyond the company's reach – from clubs and societies for scuba diving, gardening and public speaking to breast cancer support groups, bible study groups and single parents' groups.

Joanna Foster, chair of the National Work–Life Forum in the UK, a group of 70 organisations committed to improving the work-life balance of UK employees, is sceptical about why employers are offering such a huge variety of benefits. 'It seems to me some of these companies are just trying to seduce people into working harder and longer,' she says. 'What people really need is discretionary time. People feel devoured by work. Things like aromatherapy, massage and delicious meals all make work time a bit more pleasant. But they are short-term and employers need to help to improve employees' lives outside work.'

However, Arthur Friedson, vice-president of Coworker Services at Nasdaq-listed CDW Computer Centers, which came 11th in *Fortune* magazine's list this year for providing a startling array of perks ranging from childcare facilities to free turkeys at Christmas and a 'mom's corner' for breastfeeding, believes that perks serve a purpose beyond increasing productivity. 'We are a business and not a philanthropic organisation, but things like dry cleaning facilities and pre-prepared dinners are not designed to extend working hours but to give employees more time to themselves and their families. We have to attract and retain people at a time when there is nearly full employment. That's why we want to be known as a good employer.'

Copyright © The Financial Times Limited, 2000. Reproduced with permission.

Discussion questions

1   How far do you agree with the view that benefits packages are provided in order to encourage people to work harder?

2   What other purposes might a company have in providing elaborate packages such as those described in the article?

3   What new benefits would you like to see offered by your employer? What purpose would they serve from a management perspective?

Feedback

1   *How far do you agree with the view that benefits packages are provided in order to encourage people to work harder?*

One view of this article is a big 'so what?' The assumption seems to be that employers should be providing benefits to employees for entirely altruistic reasons. The discovery that there are business reasons behind it is greeted with a gasp of surprised horror. If this is so, the assumption could be seen as naive. Organisations provide benefits, just as they design other parts of the pay package, in order to meet their objectives. Some of these are HR-related, such as the need to attract and retain staff, the need to motivate them, to increase their commitment and to encourage hard work.

An alternative view, for which there is some research evidence, sees benefits in part as being offered for paternalistic reasons. The advantage to the employer is relatively slight, but they are necessary for employees and can be provided more cheaply and efficiently by employers than outside providers. Pension schemes are certainly sometimes justified in this way.

2   *What other purposes might a company have in providing elaborate packages such as those described in the article?*

- Attracting staff.

- Retaining staff.

- Raising job satisfaction levels.

- Because senior managers (who decide what to include) benefit from the packages themselves.

- Because employees want them and they are relatively inexpensive to provide.

3 *What new benefits would you like to see offered by your employer? What purpose would they serve from a management perspective?*

Answers here are clearly going to be organisation-specific. Hopefully students will be able both to identify suitable forms of benefit AND to articulate a business case for their introduction.

CHAPTER 38 INTERACTIVE SKILL: NEGOTIATION

The material in this chapter is the negotiation process, where the approach is basically similar, whether it be finding a resolution to political differences in Northern Ireland or the Balkans, or sorting out a disagreement about Saturday overtime in a small print shop. We take readers through all elements of the negotiation process, focusing particularly on effective preparation and the formulation of strategies and tactics. Our focus is on collective negotiation, but the principles are as relevant to negotiation with individuals, a topic we deal with specifically towards the end.

Additional teaching material

For a session on the practical aspects of negotiation it will help to review some of the earlier material on collective bargaining, so as to set the context for the early part of the chapter. Then make a careful introduction centred on the notion of conflict, its benefits and drawbacks.

Suggested teaching activities are as follows:

1   Try Activity 38.1 with the group, if necessary referring back to the British Airways case at the end of Part VI.

2   Run the first of the two exercises for which briefing is provided below, using two members of the group (primed beforehand) who are known for always wanting to have a say on everything. Keep it brief, but ask them to carry out the 'negotiation' in front of the rest of the group.

3   Run the Exercise 38.2, with a comprehensive concluding discussion and analysis.

4   Review the ideas in Oncken's 'freedom scale' and Fisher and Ury's four basic rules.

Exercise 38.1

You need a close friend to help you, but it is probably better not to do this exercise with a spouse: either it will be hopelessly unreal, or the negotiating behaviours will subject the relationship to needless strain.

Identify a valuable possession that you might be willing to sell for a suitable price – house, car, stereo system – and that your friend might be willing to buy from you. A realistic, albeit hypothetical, willingness on both sides is a necessary feature of selecting the possession to be 'sold'. Plan your approach for negotiating the sale, including objectives, target points and resistance points. Ask your friend to carry out similar preparation as a prospective buyer. Conduct the negotiations, attempting to avoid simple haggling about the price. When you reach potential agreement or failure to agree, discuss your feelings about the experience.

Exercise 38.2

The above exercise was relatively easy as there was only one person on each side, either party could abandon the negotiations and negotiate with someone else, and the issue in dispute was the

171

simple question of price. Also the negotiators were representing only themselves. This next exercise gets a little nearer the real thing by involving more people and more issues, but is inevitably a more artificial situation.

You need three friends, A to negotiate with you, B to be represented by you and C to be represented by your adversary. Although each of you is playing a role, try to avoid play-acting as far as possible. Dissuade A, for instance, from being deliberately bloody-minded and speaking with a Liverpool accent in order to play the part of a caricature shop steward.

You all need to read Document I. Your adversary (A) represents the members of Y Union in the plant.

Now:

1　B consults with your friend C to determine three matters they would like on the agenda for a meeting with you.

2　You have similar consultations with friend B.

3　You agree an agenda for negotiations with friend A.

4　You and B finalise your objectives; A and C finalise theirs.

5　You and A conduct negotiations, while B and C observe silently and unobtrusively.*

6　You and A reach agreement, or fail to agree, and then discuss the process with B and C.

*It is important that the observers influence the progress of negotiations as little as possible. Chuckles, sharp intakes of breath and solemn shakes of the head can quickly wreck the learning experience. As far as possible observers should be out of view of the negotiators in this exercise.

Document 1

You are being moved to be general manager of a subsidiary manufacturing plant that has had three different general managers in the last eight months. You have been told of the following major problems:

1　There is a rising rate of staff turnover on the shop floor. To maintain the complement of 420 people on production, 230 new recruits have been engaged in the last six months. In the previous six months 163 were recruited. The local level of unemployment has remained unaltered at 9 per cent.

2　Demand for the product fluctuates with a lead-time for delivery of 4–6 weeks after orders are placed. You can see no possibility of smoothing this fluctuation. The present method of coping is to rely on overtime when demand is high and to turn a blind eye to 'sickness' absence when things are slack. You have been told that the men like the overtime and the young married women like the 'sickness' absence, so it is quite a convenient arrangement.

3   Twenty-seven maintenance craftsmen and associated skilled personnel are all members of Union X. The remaining shop floor employees are represented by Union Y, although only 40–50 per cent are members. There have been seven stoppages in recent months due to breakdowns in negotiations about incentive payments. Union Z has begun recruiting members among white collar staff, who have objected to plans for harmonisation of terms and conditions between themselves and the shop floor personnel.

PART 7 CASE STUDY FEEDBACK

This case is set in the context of financial services, so some members of the group may be able to make perceptive comments from that angle. (If varied financial arrangements are your stock in trade, then you are more likely to be interested in applying those principles to your own situation.)

Our suggested answers to the set questions are:

1   (a) Salary is the basis of security and provides the greatest flexibility to the salary earner, who can use the money for whatever he or she wishes.

     (b) Salary is the basis for many benefits, especially pension and sick pay.

     (c) Salary is the main yardstick of relative worth in the labour market. It is not only the source of self-esteem, it is the main indicator to prospective employers.

2   (a) Administrative costs rise, but these become less of a problem with good computer packages for personnel administration.

     (b) You are able to give people what they want, but you may be confused about where they are relative to each other.

     (c) By providing tailored arrangements you may succeed in keeping people who cannot find equal tailoring elsewhere.

.

MULTIPLE-CHOICE QUESTIONS AND ANSWERS

Chapter 1 The nature of human resource management

1.1

Which of the following statements about human resource management is correct?

A   There is an increasing emphasis on the administration of contracts of employment.
B   There is an increasing emphasis on 'the organisation as entity'.
C   There is an increasing emphasis on 'the organisation as process'.
D   There is a decreasing emphasis on 'the contract for performance'.

Answer: C

1.2

Which of the following correctly lists the four principal types of of HRM objective?

A   administration, legal, performance, economic
B   administration, change management, staffing, performance
C   change management, economic, staffing, commitment
D   change management, legal, staffing, performance

Answer: B

1.3

Which of the following HRM/personnel roles has the longest history?

A   social reformer
B   consensus negotiator
C   acolyte of benevolence
D   humane bureaucrat

Answer: A

1.4

Which stage in the development of the HRM/personnel role is chiefly associated with the 1960s?

A   the humane bureaucrat
B   the consensus negotiator
C   organisation man
D   manpower analyst

Answer: C

1.5

What is being described here?

An approach to the management of people which is associated with management interests and puts emphasis on planning, monitoring and control.

A human resource management
B personnel management
C manpower analysis
D line management

Answer: A

Chapter 2 Current issues in human resource management

2.1

What is being described here?

An expectation, on the part of both management and staff, that long-term employment in the organisation is unlikely but that employees can expect developmental opportunities.

A the old psychological contract
B the new psychological contract
C a cost reduction HR stategy
D an added-value HR stategy

Answer: B

2.2

After how many months' continuous service do UK employees gain the legal right not to be unfairly dismissed?

A 3 months
B 6 months
C 12 months
D 24 months

Answer: C

2.3

What is being described here?

A relationship in which the role of the trade union is not one of perpetual opposition but is instead supportive and constructive of legitimate management initiatives.

A   a collective agreement
B   a stakeholder agreement
C   a single-union agreement
D   a partnership agreement

Answer: D

2.4

Which writer argued that corporate social responsibility should be limited to profit making within the boundaries of the law?

A   Katz
B   Friedman
C   Pfeffer
D   Guest

Answer: B

2.5

What is being described here?

The view that there are certain HR practices and approaches to their operation which will invariably help an organisation in achieving competitive advantage.

A   a best practice perspective
B   a best fit perspective
C   an ethical perspective
D   a resource-based perspective

Answer: A

Chapter 3 Strategic human resource management

3.1

In which of the five types of relationship between organisational strategy and HR strategy does organisational strategy have the greatest dominance over HR strategy?

A   separation
B   fit
C   dialogue
D   holistic
E   HR driven

Answer: B

3.2

Which of the following is NOT a part of Mintzberg's (1994) view of the 'formation of strategy'?

A   Intended strategy is changed by events.
B   Realised strategy is different from the initial vision.
C   Strategy can be formulated in advance and can be achieved if carefully planned.
D   Strategy can only be seen in retrospect.

Answer: C

3.3

Guest (1989b) identified four policy goals of HRM. Which of the following is NOT one of Guest's four policy goals?

A   strategic integration
B   commitment
C   flexibility
D   continuous learning

Answer: D

3.4

Which of the following three criticisms apply to the Fombrun, Tichy and Devanna model of HR strategy?

A   It focuses on content, not process.
B   It assumes a one-way relationship between organisational strategy and HR strategy.
C   It assumes a rational strategy formulation approach.
D   It is unitarist and neglects differential employee interests.

Answers: B, C and D

3.5

Which of the following does NOT apply to the resource-based approach to HR strategy?

A   It focuses on human capital.
B   It views the cost of developing the human resource as a capital expense.
C   It is concerned with skills, knowledge, attitudes and competencies.
D   It is concerned with promoting sustained competitive advantage.

Answer: B

Chapter 4 Strategic aspects of organisation

4.1

What was lacking in Sir Clive Sinclair's development of the electric car?

A   proper technical specification
B   financial investment
C   supply of materials
D   industrial relations procedures
E   appropriate structures and management processes

Answer: E

4.2

Evangelisation as a method of co-ordination works through which *three* of the following?

A   shared beliefs
B   mission statements
C   apostles
D   parables
E   job enrichment

Answers: A, C and D

4.3

Tom Peters writes that 'the long-range strategic plan, of voluminous length' is:

A   more essential than ever
B   needed in most businesses
C   too long
D   based on insufficient evidence
E   less useful than before

Answer: E

4.4

What are the three problems cited of expanding by acquiring a business in a different country?

Answers:

rivalry
distorted perceptions
resource allocation

4.5

What was the finding of Pascale (1978) about how Japanese managers operate in the USA?

A   They used communication in the same way as the Americans.
B   They used more face-to-face communication.
C   They used more vertical communication.
D   They were more formal.
E   They ignored feedback.

Answer: A

Chapter 5 Planning: jobs and people

5.1

Which of the following does Mintzberg (1994) consider to be part of strategic *planning*?

A   collecting and analysing internal and external data
B   asking difficult and challenging questions
C   articulating a not-too-precise vision of the future
D   programming the vision so that it becomes achievable
E   ensuring co-ordination and encouraging everyone to pull in the same direction

Answer: C

5.2

In relation to human resource planning, work study is usually classified as:

A an objective method of analysing employee demand
B a subjective method of analysing employee demand
C an objective method of analysing employee supply
D a subjective method of analysing employee supply

Answer: A

5.3

The annual labour turnover index is sometimes referred to as:

A cohort analysis
B stability index
C percentage wastage rate
D retention profile

Answer: C

5.4

The census method is normally used as a method of:

A analysing staff leaving the organisation
B succession planning
C analysing internal movements
D reconciling supply and demand projections

Answer: A

5.5

HR planning should ideally be carried out as:

A an annual process
B a bi-annual process
C a five-yearly process
D a continuous process

Answer: D

Chapter 6 Organisational design

6.1

From the list of Handy's (1993) four organisational forms (based on Harrison 1972) identify which is the most appropriate label for the following definition:

This form of organisation emphasises central power, usually with one dominant person in the centre.

A entrepreneurial
B bureaucratic
C matrix
D independence

Answer: A

6.2

The notion of bureaucracy is based on the original work of:

A Henri Fayol
B Charles Handy
C Meredith Belbin
D Max Weber

Answer: D

6.3

BPR stands for:

A business production reporting
B business process re-engineering
C business procedures re-engineering
D business production re-engineering
E British production rates

Answer: B

6.4

When the words 'organisational culture' are used as a metaphor, this refers to culture as something which the organisation:

A is
B has
C uses
D changes

Answer: A

6.5

Schein (1984) defined three levels of organisational culture. The deepest level is:

A values
B behaviour
C technology
D basic assumptions
E artefacts

Answer: D

Chapter 7 Communication and information

7.1

Which *two* of the following statements apply to the concept of cognitive dissonance as described by Festinger (1957)?

A We find it hard to accept information which conflicts with our established beliefs.
B Noise from the environment distracts us from making sense of what we hear.
C We sometimes distort the message we hear so that it fits with our view of the world.

Answers: A and C

7.2

Barriers to effective communication can be located in three key areas. One area is social/environmental, and another is the recipient. Which is the third key area?

A other listeners
B the sender
C the message

Answer: B

7.3

The term absence rate means:

A the number of days' absence per year of all employees added together
B the above divided by the number of potential working days and multiplied by 100
C the number of spells of absence over a year

Answer: A

7.4

The 1998 Data Protection Act will be fully in force by:

A 23 October 2001
B 24 October 2001
C 24 October 2007
D 24 October 2010

Answer: C

7.5

The Data Protection Acts of 1984 and 1998 each incorporate a series of principles. Which *two* of the following statements about the principles are correct?

A There were eight principles in the 1984 Act and three additional principles in the 1998 Act.
B There were five principles in the 1984 Act and eight principles in the 1998 Act.
C Five of the principles in the 1998 Act are similar to the principles of the 1984 Act and three of the principles in the 1998 Act represent significant developments.
D There were eight principles in the 1984 Act and eight principles in the 1998 Act.
E There were eight principles in the 1984 Act and these have been reduced to five in the 1998 Act, three of which are significant developments.

Answers: C and D

Chapter 8 Interactive skill: chairing meetings

8.1

The chapter gives four examples of meetings that personnel specialists have to chair. What are they?

Answers:

selection panels
meetings with union officials
health and safety committees
job evaluation groups

8.2

What are the five check questions for preparing for a meeting?

Answers:

Who should attend the meeting?
What is the brief or the terms of reference?
What should the agenda be?
What about physical location and arrangements?
What is the meeting for?

8.3

What are the five points which, it is suggested, the person chairing the meeting should attend to, in order to ensure it is properly conducted?

Answers:

How can contributions be stimulated and controlled?
Bringing people in.
Keeping it going.
What about your own input?
Winding it up.

8.4

What are the two features of follow-up?

Answers:

Minutes or report
Implementation of proposals

Chapter 9 Strategic aspects of resourcing

9.1

Which of the following statements is true as regards labour markets in the UK during the coming decades?

A   There will be a shortage of older workers.
B   There will be a shortage of younger workers.
C   Demand for skilled workers will fall.
D   Demand for female workers will fall.

Answer: B

9.2

Which of the following occupational groups has grown most in recent years?

A   Professional and managerial
B   Clerical and secretarial
C   Skilled manual
D   Unskilled manual

Answer: A

9.3

What is being described here?

A type of labour market in which employees perceive that it is necessary for them regularly to move from employer to employer, building up a portfolio of experience on which to draw.

A   a craft market
B   an unstructured market
C   a tight market
D   a national market

Answer: A

9.4

What is being described here?

An approach to staffing which makes use of alternatives to traditional, permanent employment through the use of short-term contracts.

A financial flexibility
B functional flexibility
C temporal flexibility
D numerical flexibility

Answer: D

9.5

What is being described here?

An approach to staffing which moves away from the 9–5, 40-hour week through the use of part-time contracts and flexible working hours.

A financial flexibility
B functional flexibility
C temporal flexibility
D numerical flexibility

Answer: C

Chapter 10   Contracts, contractors and consultants

10.1

Which of the following legal rights are enjoyed by all workers in the UK, whatever their employment status?

A equal pay for equal work
B minimum notice periods
C time off for public duties
D statutory sick pay

Answer: A

10.2

Which of the following is a common law duty owed by all employers to their employees?

A   a duty to provide training
B   a duty to recognise trade unions
C   a duty to provide work
D   a duty to provide meals

Answer: C

10.3

What percentage of UK employees work on a part-time basis?

A   13.5%
B   22.5%
C   28.5%
D   32.5%

Answer: C

10.4

What is being described here?

A method of reducing the working week by extending the working day, so that people regularly work the same number of hours but on fewer days.

A   a flexible hours contract
B   an annual hours contract
C   a zero hours contract
D   a compressed hours contract

Answer: D

10.5

According to Duncan Wood's (1985) research, what is the most common reason for employing consultants in the field of HRM?

A   to provide specialist expertise not available within the client organisation
B   to provide an independent view
C   to act as a catalyst for change
D   to provide extra resources to meet temporary requirements

Answer: A

Chapter 11 Recruitment

11.1

Which of the following is a common reason for using headhunters in recruitment?

A It is less expensive than advertising a position.
B It allows confidential channels of communication to be opened to individuals working for competitors.
C It produces a good cross-section of applicants.
D It leads to the appointment of individuals who stay for longer periods of time.

Answer: B

11.2

What is being described here?

A firm which books advertising space, draws up recruitment advertisements, places them in newspapers/journals and evaluates the results.

A an employment agency
B an executive search consultancy
C a selection consultancy
D a recruitment advertising agency

Answer: D

11.3

Which of the following national newspapers has had the greatest share of recruitment advertising in recent years?

A *The Daily Telegraph*
B *Guardian*
C *The Times*
D *The Sunday Times*

Answer: B

11.4

What is being described here?

The process by which employers advertising jobs on the web get bombarded with applications from thousands of interested jobseekers.

A   flooding
B   bombing
C   spamming
D   jetting

Answer: C

11.5

Which of the following reasons given for screening out candidates prior to shortlisting could be open to legal challenge?

A   handwritten applications
B   unemployed applicants
C   applications from non-graduates
D   unmarried applicants

Answer: D

Chapter 12 Selection methods and decisions

12.1

In relation to selection testing, the term 'reliability' is used to mean the extent to which

A   the test can predict subsequent job performance
B   the test can predict length of service
C   the test consistently measures whatever it does measure
D   the test predicts employees who will be reliable

Answer: C

12.2

The predetermination of appropriate competencies is a critical part of the assessment centre as at the centre the observers will record:

A standards
B behaviours
C potential
D personality

Answer: B

12.3

Which of the following correlation co-efficients indicate the strongest positive relationship between test results and performance criteria?

A +0.25
B +0.42
C +0.1
D -0.61
E +0.55

Answer: E

12.4

In the context of selection the term biodata means:

A health check related to the demands of the job
B checking eligibility for entry into the pension and private health scheme
C historical and verifiable pieces of information about an individual
D a check on absence records and previous sickness

Answer: C

Chapter 13 Staff retention

13.1

Which of the following areas of employment persistently records the lowest levels of staff turnover?

A sales
B retailing
C manufacturing
D emergency services

Answer: D

13.2

What is being described here?

A situation in which poorer performers resign and are replaced by employees with greater ability.

A functional turnover
B dysfunctional turnover
C high turnover
D unplanned turnover

Answer: A

13.3

What is being described here?

A face-to-face meting held with employees after they have handed in their resignations.

A a grievance interview
B an exit interview
C a performance appraisal
D an attitude survey

Answer: B

13.4

Which of the following statements on pay and staff retention is correct?

A Raising pay invariably reduces staff turnover.
B Raising pay does not deter unhappy employees from leaving.
C Reducing pay has little effect on staff turnover.
D The lower the pay, the higher the turnover.

Answer: B

13.5

On average, which of these groups has the shortest job tenure in the UK?

A men with children
B men without children
C women with children
D women without children

Answer: C

Chapter 14 Ending the contract

14.1

What percentage of dismissed employees in the UK are estimated to bring claims of unfair dismissal against their former employers?

A 1–4%
B 5–10%
C 11–15%
D 16–20%

Answer: B

14.2

What is being described here?

A situation in which an employee's dismissal breaches statute (i.e. an Act of Parliament).

A wrongful dismissal
B unjust dismissal
C unfair dismissal
D constructive dismissal

Answer: C

14.3

Which of the following reasons for dismissal is considered 'automatically unfair' by employment tribunals?

A   disobedience
B   illness
C   trade union membership
D   redundancy

Answer: C

14.4

Which of the following reasons for dismissal is defined as 'potentially fair' by employment tribunals?

A   ill health
B   pregnancy
C   trade union membership
D   disability

Answer: A

14.5

In the absence of any specific contractual term, how many weeks' notice is an employee entitled to having completed 15 years of serrvice?

A   4 weeks
B   8 weeks
C   12 weeks
D   15 weeks

Answer: C

Chapter 15 Interactive skill: selection interviewing

15.1

What are the *three* main purposes of the selection interview?

Answers:

To predict how well the applicants would perform in the job.
To facilitate the candidate's decision making.
To give candidates a fair hearing.

15.2

What are the *four* main criticisms of the typical selection interview?

Answers:

Interviewers deciding in the first few minutes of the interview.
Interviewers prejudging on the basis of the application form and the candidate's appearance.
Interviewers placing most weight on unfavourable evidence.
Interviewers betraying their decision to the candidate.

15.3
What are the *four* main types of selection interview strategy?

Answers:

Frank and friendly
Problem-solving
Biographical
Stress

15.4

What are the *four* aspects of the setting for a selection interview suggested in Chapter 15?

Answers:

The room should be suitable for a private conversation.
The extent to which a desk acts as a barrier should be reduced.
Visitors and telephone calls should be avoided.
It should be clear to the candidates where they are to sit.

15.5.

What are the *six* arguments given in favour of structuring interviews?

Answers:

Candidates expect interviews to be stuctured.
It helps ensure that all relevant areas are covered.
It looks professional.
It allows effective time management.
The application form can be used as a memory aid.
It eases comparisons among the candidates.

15.6.

Which *six* broad aspects of interview method are described?

Answers:

Observation
Listening
Directing the candidate
Making notes on application or CV
Data exchange
Closing

Chapter 16 Stategic aspects of performance

16.1

The term 'behavioural commitment' has been defined as:

A   making sure one's behaviours match company norms
B   remaining with the company and continuing to pursue its objectives
C   being committed to the behaviours attached to the competency specification for one's job
D   behaving in line with the prevailing culture

Answer: B

16.2

Kaplan and Norton (1992) suggested performance measures should be based around four different perspectives. Which of the following is not one of the four?

A   financial measures
B   supplier measures
C   internal business measures
D   innovation and learning perspective

Answer: B

16.3

The 'bundles' approach to high performance falls most naturally into which approach to HR strategy?

A   universalist/best practice
B   fit/contingency
C   resource-based view

Answer: A

16.4

To whom is the following quotation attributed?

> Our concern should be less about the precise policy mix in the 'bundle' and more about how and when organisations manage the HR side of change.

A Pfeffer
B Purcell
C Walton
D Guest

Answer: B

Chapter 17 Organisational performance

17.1

Wilkinson *et al.* (1998) identify four stages of quality management. The fourth stage is:

A Japanisation and quality circles
B Emphasis on customer service
C Quality push in the public sector
D Statistical quality control

Answer: C

17.2

To whom is the following quotation, defining a learning organisation, attributed?

An organisation which facilitates the learning of all its members and continually transforms itself.

A Easterby-Smith
B Pedler, Burgoyne and Boydell
C Popper and Lipshitz
D Argyris and Schon

Answer: B

17.3

Pedler, Burgoyne and Boydell (1991) produced a 'blueprint' of a learning company. Which of the following characteristics is not one of the 11 that they identified?

A a learning approach to strategy
B informating
C reward flexibility
D high levels of formal training

Answer: D

17.4

Senge (1990) identified five vital dimensions in building organisations which can learn. Which of the following is not one of the five?

A stewardship
B systems thinking
C mental models
D shared visions

Answer: A

Chapter 18 Managing individual performance

18.1

Which *three* of the following are stages in the basic performance cycle as illustrated in Chapter 18 on p. 298?

A rewarding performance
B planning performance
C reviewing performance
D supporting performance

Answers: B, C and D

18.2

Fletcher and Williams (1985) identified conflicting roles that line managers have to play in the appraisal process. Which *two* are they?

A judge
B rater
C developer
D helper

Answers: A and D

18.3

BARS stands for:

A   behaviourally actioned reward system
B   behaviourally anchored rating scale
C   behavioural assessment reporting system
D   battery of appraisal rating scales

Answer: B

18.4

Which of the following statements is correct?

A   The use of a performance management system implies that there must be a direct link between performance and pay.
B   The use of performance-related pay means that a performance management system must be in place.
C   The use of a performance management system excludes a link between performance and pay.
D   Most, but not all, performance management systems link pay with performance.

Answer: D

18.5

360° feedback is:

A   continuous feedback
B   feedback on all aspects of the employee
C   multiple-source feedback
D   structured feedback from peers

Answer: C

Chapter 19 Team performance

19.1

Which of the following statements does not reflect Moxon's definition of a team?

A   Members have a common purpose.
B   Agreed norms and values regulate behaviour.
C   Team members need independent roles.
D   There is a recognition of team identity.

Answer: C

19.2

Whose research resulted in the framework of nine 'team roles'?

A   Katzenbach and Smith
B   Belbin
C   Drucker
D   Buchanan

Answer: B

19.3

The 'plant' team role is a person who:

A   offers creative and original ideas
B   asks challenging questions about the ideas of others
C   looks for patterns and tries to pull things together
D   supplies the team with a network of contacts

Answer: A

19.4

Which of the following is not one of the four stages of team development as identified by Tuckman?
A   performing
B   norming
C   reviewing
D   storming

Answer: C

Chapter 20 Leadership and motivation

20.1

One school of thought in the literature characterises the difference between leadership and management. Which *three* of the following characteristics apply to leadership rather than management:

A   path-finding
B   establish direction
C   plan and budget
D   encourage change

Answers: A, B and D

20.2

Which *three* of the following comprise Goleman's (1998) components of emotional intelligence?

A   self-awareness
B   self-regulation
C   empathy
D   therapy skills

Answers: A, B and C

20.3

Which of the following is not one of Blake and Mouton's (1964) four leadership styles?

A   country club management
B   authority-compliance management
C   supportive management
D   team management

Answer: C

20.4

Which leadership theory from Hersey and Blanchard (1988) suggests that leaders can adapt their style to meet the demands of the environment/followers?

A   contingency theory
B   situational leadership
C   the managerial grid
D   empowering leadership

Answer: B

20.5

Which *three* of the following roles does Senge (1990) suggest that leaders need to use?

A   designer
B   teacher
C   counsellor
D   steward

Answers: A, B and D

Chapter 21 Diversity: the legal framework

21.1

What is being described here?

The situation that occurs when an employer sets a 'requirement or condition' which has the effect of disadvantaging a significantly larger proportion of one sex than the other.

A   victimisation
B   direct discrimination
C   positive discrimination
D   indirect discrimination

Answer: D

21.2

Which of the following might constitute indirect sex discrimination?

A   stating in an advertisement for a secretarial position that a woman is required
B   selecting people for jobs on the basis of their height
C   selecting people for redundancy on the basis that they were married
D   failing to shortlist women of child-bearing age

Answer: B

21.3

In which of the following jobs might sex discrimination be permitted on grounds of a genuine occupational qualification?

A waiter/waitress
B doctor
C hairdresser
D model

Answer: D

21.4

Which of the following jobs is excluded from the Disability Discrimination Act?

A school teacher
B HGV driver
C prison officer
D hospital porter

Answer: C

21.5

A criminal offence is never 'spent' under the law if the sentence served is over what duration?

A 12 months
B 24 months
C 30 months
D 40 months

Answer: C

Chapter 22 Equality: equal opportunities and diversity

22.1

The New Earnings Survey (2000) found that men earn, on average, £24,298 p.a., and that women earn, on average:

A £22,430
B £20,090
C £17,556
D £16,200

Answer: C

22.2

People with a disability form what proportion of the working-age population?

A   One-fifth
B   One-eighth
C   One-tenth
D   One-twelfth

Answer: A

22.3

The provision of special support and encouragement for previously disadvantaged groups is legally acceptable in the UK. This support is termed:

A   positive discrimination
B   positive action
C   reverse discrimination
D   affirmative action

Answer: B

22.4

Managing diversity is a range of approaches with different emphases. Who identified the following four approaches: individualism, valuing differences, accommodating and utilising?

A   Miller
B   Ouseley
C   Liff
D   Kandola and Fullerton

Answer: C

22.5

LaFasto (1992) identified three stages in a conceptual model of diversity. Stage two is managing diversity and stage three is valuing diversity. What was stage one?

A   equal opportunities
B   affirmative action
C   compliance
D   creating diversity

Answer: C

Chapter 23 Interactive skill: the appraisal interview

23.1

Which *two* of the following are two contrasted motivations that drive the appraisal interview?

A   management control
B   financial control
C   legal requirement
D   equal opportunity
E   self-development

Answers: A and D

23.2

What were the different styles of appraisal interview described by the American psychologist Norman Maier (1958)?

Answers:

problem solving
tell and sell
tell and listen

23.3

Fill in the gaps using the four words given below:

the opening of the interview itself still needs care. The mood needs to be (A) … but not (B) …, as the appraisee has to be encouraged towards (C) … rather than (D …

candour
trivial
light
gamesmanship

Answers:

A   light
B   trivial
C   candour
D   gamesmanship

23.4

Put the following in the sequence recommended for the appraisal interview:

A   Factual review
B   Appraiser views
C   Problem solving
D   Appraisee views
E   Objective setting
F   Purpose and rapport

Answer: F, A, D, B, C, E

Chapter 24   Strategic aspects of development

24.1

Development has traditionally been seen as a cost rather than a/an:

A   cost saving
B   investment
C   deferred cost
D   long-term budget

Answer: B

24.2

The national training framework in the UK is known as 'voluntarist'. This means:

A   The government is limited to encouraging training.
B   Employees must not be trained unless they volunteer.
C   Large organisations volunteer to develop the national framework.
D   The government volunteers to intervene directly in training.

Answer: A

24.3

The new psychological contract promotes:

A   continued employment by the same employer
B   short-term contract working
C   employability
D   a commitment from employers not to under-recruit

Answer: C

24.4

Salaman and Mabey (1995) proposed a range of stakeholders in training and development. In their framework they identify senior managers as ... of training and development?

A funders
B sponsors
C arbiters
D facilitators

Answer: B

24.5

LSC stands for:

A learning and strategy consortium
B local skills committee
C learning and skills consortium
D learning and skills council

Answer: C

Chapter 25 Competencies, competence and NVQs

25.1

Competencies refer to:

A behaviour
B job standards
C values
D potential

Answer: A

25.2

The major contributor to the early work on behavioural competencies was:

A Berry
B Brewis
C Brittain
D Boyatzis

Answer: D

25.3

NVQs have how many levels?

A   three
B   five
C   six
D   seven

Answer: B

25.4

Which of the following is *not* one of the level three standards for managers?

A   to manage activities
B   to manage people
C   to manage information
D   to manage equality

Answer: D

25.5

Boyatzis (1982) produced five clusters of competencies. Which of the following is *not* one of the five?

A   goal and action management
B   operational management
C   leadership
D   human resource management

Answer: B

Chapter 26 Learning and development

26.1

Which of the following is *not* one of Honey and Mumford's (1989) labels for learning styles?

A   activist
B   reflector
C   theorist
D   implementer

Answer: D

26.2

Who developed a model of planned and emergent learning, identifying four types of learner as sage, warrior, adventurer and sleeper?

A Mumford
B Kolb
C Megginson
D Harrison

Answer: C

26.3

The warrior style is:

A low planned learning score, low emergent learning score
B low planned learning score, high emergent learning score
C high planned learning score, low emergent learning score
D high planned learning score, high emergent learning score

Answer: C

26.4

Which approach to development is Reg Revans (1974) most closely associated with?

A coaching
B mentoring
C action learning
D e-learning

Answer: C

26.5

A learning contract is primarily:

A a reactive approach to developing learning
B a proactive approach to developing learning
C a contract for promotion contingent on developing learning
D a contract for skills-based pay

Answer: B

Chapter 27 Career development

27.1

Who said that a portfolio career means 'exchanging full-time employment for independence'?

A   Arthur
B   Handy
C   Herriot
D   Kanter

Answer: B

27.2

Which *three* of the following apply to employees and what they offer to employers within the *old* psychological contract?

A   loyalty
B   commitment
C   continuous learning
D   adequate performance

Answers: A, B and D

27.3

What did Adamson *et al.* (1998) define as a rich CV?

A   an impressive list of job titles increasing in seniority
B   where the individual has always increased their pay from one job to the following one
C   a variety of work and non-work activities
D   a detailed CV illustrating what has been learned from each job experience

Answer: C

27.4

Who developed the concept of career anchors?

A   Mayo
B   Harrison
C   Greenhaus and Callanan
D   Schein

Answer: D

27.5

Driver (1982) identifies 'spiral careers', by which he means careers where:

A   the individual moves frequently between organisations
B   the individual is sometimes self-employed and sometimes full-time employed in rotation
C   individuals are self-employed and only work for a small number of core customers
D   the individual develops in one area of the organisation for a time and then moves to another area(s) and develops

Answer: D

Chapter 28 Interactive skill: presentation and teaching

28.1

What do the letters CRAMP stand for?

Answer:

comprehension
reflex learning
attitude development
memory training
procedural learning

28.2

What were the *five* stages of learning capacity identified by Quinn (1988)?

Answer:

1   the novice
2   the advanced beginner
3   competency
4   proficiency
5   expert

28.3

Practising routine 1, then routine 2, then routines 1 + 2, then routine 3, then routines 1 + 2 + 3, is the basis of:

A   cumulative part method
B   simplification
C   comprehension
D   memorisation
E   progressive part method

Answer: E

28.4

What are the *four* suggested ways of organising the material in the main body of a presentation?

Answer:

chronological sequence
known to unknown/simple to complex
problem to solution
comparison

28.5

What are the *two* basic types of notes for a presentation?

Answer:

headlines
script

Chapter 29 Strategic aspects of employee relations

29.1

According to the Workplace Employee Relations Survey, what percentage of employees believe the employee relations climate in their place of work to be poor?

A   2%
B   13%
C   21%
D   42%

Answer: C

29.2

To the nearest million, what is the current total level of trade union membership in the UK?

A 3 million
B 8 million
C 12 million
D 16 million

Answer: B

29.3

What is being described here?

A pragmatic approach to trade union activity which seeks to gain influence in organisations by working with, rather than in opposition to managements.

A business unionism
B a closed shop
C employee involvement
D collective bargaining

Answer: A

29.4

Which 'category of consent' is being described here?

A situation in which employees form trade unions, agreeing to obey management instructions as long as their grievances are dealt with.

A normative
B organised
C consultative
D participative

Answer: B

29.5

What is being described here?

A form of employee involvement which involves groups of around a dozen employees meeting regularly to generate ideas aimed at improving productivity.

A   team briefing
B   quality circles
C   team working
D   European Works Councils

Answer: B

Chapter 30 Recognition and consultation

30.1

Which of the following legal rights accrues to a union which is recognised in an organisation?

A   the right to organise strike action
B   the right to be consulted about collective redundancies
C   the right to information about business strategy
D   the right for stewards to spend one day a week on union duties

Answer: B

30.2

What is being described here?

A situation in which management reduce the scope or number of decision-making areas which are subject to collective bargaining.

A   partial derecognition
B   full derecognition
C   new style agreement
D   single-table bargaining

Answer: A

30.3

Which of the following is commonly associated with single-union agreements?

A   no-strike clauses
B   strict demarcation
C   a closed shop
D   co-determination

Answer: A

30.4

Which body is responsible for hearing trade union recognition claims brought under the Employment Relations Act 1999?

A   ACAS
B   European Court of Justice
C   Employment Tribunal
D   Central Arbitration Committee

Answer: D

30.5

What is being described here?

A process by which a consultative forum is used by managers principally to inform employees about decisions that have already been taken.

A   joint consultative committee
B   European Works Council
C   pseudo-consultation
D   team briefing

Answer: C

Chapter 31 Health, safety and welfare

31.1

According to the Health and Safety Executive, what is the total annual cost to employers attributable to injuries sustained at work?

A £2.5 million
B £25 million
C £250 million
D £2.5 billion

Answer: D

31.2

What is being described here?

An order served by a health and safety inspector requiring that an organisation ceases carrying out an activity until specified remedial action has been taken.

A an improvement notice
B a prohibition notice
C a safety mandate
D a protection mandate

Answer: B

31.3

Which of the following legislative instruments established the contemporary regulatory framework for health and safety at work?

A The Factories Act 1961
B The Offices, Shops and Railway Premises Act 1963
C The Health and Safety at Work etc. Act 1974
D The Control of Substances Hazardous to Health Regulations 1988

Answer: C

31.4

According to research into health and safety training, which of the following techniques is most effective?

A poster campaigns
B discussion groups
C disciplinary action
D role playing

Answer: D

31.5

What is being described here?

An employer-sponsored initiative to help employees relieve stress and develop healthier lifestyles.

A a positive health programme
B an occupational health service
C a career break scheme
D a counselling service

Answer: A

Chapter 32 Grievance and discipline

32.1

Milgram's (1974) experiments were advertised to potential subjects as dealing with which of the following:

A study skills
B discipline and punishment
C memory and learning
D obedience
E resistance to punishment

Answer: C

32.2

What were the *six* factors that Milgram (1974) said laid the groundwork for obedience to authority?

Answers:

Family
Institutional setting
Rewards
Perception of authority
Entry into the authority system
The overarching ideology

32.3

What are the *five* features of the framework of organisational justice?

Answers:

Awareness of culture and appropriateness of style
Rules
Ensuring that the rules are kept
Managerial discipline
Procedural sequence
Penalties

32.4

Figure 32.4 in the text (p. 540) suggests up to five potential steps in disciplinary procedure. What are they?

Answers:

Verbal warning
Written warning
Final written warning
Transfer, demotion or suspension
Dismissal

Chapter 33 Interactive skill: grievance and disciplinary interviewing

33.1

Who is reported to have advocated an approach to management based on integration and self-control?

A   Douglas McGregor
B   Charles Atlas
C   Ewen McGregor
D   Henry Newbolt Smith
E   Francis Chichester

Answer: A

33.2

What is suggested as the appropriate setting for the later stages of procedure?

A   In a pub, over a pie and a pint.
B   At the offices of a professional counsellor.
C   In the company canteen.
D   In the large, impressive office of a senior manager.
E   At a free desk in an open-plan office.

Answer: D

33.3

How are the phases of a grievance interview summarised?

Answer:

Manager states subject of grievance.
Employee agrees with statement.
Employee states case.
Manager questions for clarification.
Manager re-states grievance.
Employee agrees or corrects.

33.4

What are the second, third and fourth possible moves to disengagement?

Answer:

2 Persuasion
3 Disapproval
4 Penalties

33.5

What are Eric Harvey's (1987) three simple steps in 'positive discipline'?

Answer:

1 Warn the employee orally.
2 Warn the employee in writing.
3 If steps 1 and 2 fail, give the employee a day off, with pay.

Chapter 34 Strategic aspects of payment

34.1

Which employee objective for the contract of payment is being described here?

A concern with ensuring that one's rate of pay is reasonable when compared to that of comparable groups.

A recognition
B relativities
C felt-fair
D rights

Answer: B

34.2

Which of the following statements concerning employer objectives in payment systems is correct?

A   In practice the level of pay offered by an organisation has little effect on its reputation as an employer.
B   Incentives are primarily used to motivate manual workers and sales staff.
C   Incentive schemes based on quantity are inappropriate where the quality of output is important.
D   Recently there has been less emphasis on 'risk money' in the remuneration of senior executives.

Answer: C

34.3

What is being described here?

A group of employers, often based in the same locality, who agree to exchange pay information for mutual benefit.

A   a salary club
B   a wage association
C   a compensation circle
D   a pay databank

Answer: A

34.4

Which of the following elements of a payment package is classed as 'variable'?

A   company car
B   pension
C   basic pay
D   overtime

Answer: D

34.5

What is being described here?

A gratuitous payment made by the employer that is not directly earned by the employee.

A   bonus
B   premium
C   incentive
D   plussage

Answer: A

Chapter 35   Job evaluation

35.1

What is being described here?

The difference in the level of pay between the bottom rung of adjacent ladders in a salary group.

A   span
B   overlap
C   relativity
D   differential

Answer: D

35.2

What is being described here?

An approach to determining pay rates which compares each job with others in terms of the skills, knowledge and experience needed to carry it out effectively.

A   analytical job evaluation
B   non-analytical job evaluation
C   proprietary job evaluation
D   structural job evaluation

Answer: A

35.3

What is being described here?

The process by which an individual's rate of pay is protected following a job evaluation exercise which finds their job to be overpaid.

A whole job analysis
B weighting
C green circling
D red circling

Answer: D

35.4

What is being described here?

A defence available to employers faced with an equal value claim by which a difference in pay rates between individual employees is justified.

A a Bromley defence
B a Danfoss defence
C genuine material factor
D genuine occupational qualification

Answer: C

35.5

What is being described here?

An approach to payment which makes use of ladders and steps but which also provides scope for variation in rates dependent on skill, performance and external differentials.

A analytical job evaluation
B non-analytical job evaluation
C broadbanding
D job familes

Answer: C

Chapter 36 – Incentives

36.1

Which of the following statements about the extent of incentives in the UK is correct?

A   The proportion of employees receiving incentive payments is increasing.
B   The proportion of employees receiving incentive payments is falling.
C   The proportion of employees receiving incentive payments is stable.
D   It is unclear what proportion of employees is receiving incentive payments.

Answer: D

36.2

What is being described here?

An incentive payment system which rewards employees provided they maintain a predetermined and agreed level of working.

A   piecework
B   individual time saving
C   measured daywork
D   gainsharing

Answer: C

36.3

According to Armstrong and Murlis (1998), what is the lowest level of performance-related payment it is necessary to give in order for a system to have incentive effects?

A   3%
B   5%
C   8%
D   10%

Answer: A

36.4

Which of the following statements about the academic judgement on performance-related pay is most accurate?

A unfavourable
B fairly favourable
C very favourable
D mixed

Answer: A

36.5

What is being described here?

A payment system which rewards groups of employees with incentive payments when they put in place initiatives which reduce costs.

A flexible benefits
B gainsharing
C profit sharing
D merit pay

Answer: B

Chapter 37 Pensions and benefits

37.1

What is being described here?

A system which allows employees a degree of choice in how their total payment package is made up.

A a cafeteria system
B a pick-and-mix system
C a self-design system
D a pliable system

Answer: A

37.2

What is being described here?

An occupational pension scheme which pays a pension based on the number of years' service and the salary at the date of retirement.

A   SERPS
B   a defined benefit scheme
C   a defined contribution scheme
D   a hybrid scheme

Answer: B

37.3

What level of pension would an employee receive if he/she was a member of a sixtieths final salary pension scheme, had forty years' pensionable service and was earning £30,000 a year at the date of retirement?

A   £15,000 per year
B   £20,000 per year
C   £25,000 per year
D   £30,000 per year

Answer: B

37.4

What percentage of those entitled to a company car in the UK choose instead to take a cash alternative?

A   18%
B   28%
C   38%
D   48%

Answer: A

37.5

Which formula is typically used in public sector organisations to calculate entitlement to occupational sick pay?

A   six months' full pay
B   six months' half pay
C   three months full pay followed by three months' half pay
D   six months full pay, followed by six months' half pay

Answer: D

Chapter 38 Interactive skill: negotiation

38.1

What is described in Chapter 38 as the main source of industrial relations conflict?

A   social class divisions
B   poor productivity
C   low pay
D   divergence of interests between managers and non-managers
E   politicians interfering in business

Answer: D

38.2

What *six* potential benefits of such conflict are described in Chapter 38?

Answer:

introducing new rules
modifying the goals
clash of values
competitiveness
organisational tradition
understanding of respective positions

38.3

What *five* bargaining strategies are described?

Answer:

avoidance
smoothing
forcing
compromise
confrontation

38.4

What *five* aspects of bargaining tactics are described?

Answer:

resolution or accommodation
tension level
power balance
synchronising
openness

38.5

What *six* stages in the negotiation itself are described?

Answer:

setting
challenge and defiance
thrust and parry
decision making
recapitulation
written statement